Fatima Gaddar

Birth Rituals In The Amazigh Culture And Socio-Economic Development

Fatima Gaddar

Birth Rituals In The Amazigh Culture And Socio-Economic Development

The Case of Ayt Merghad

LAP LAMBERT Academic Publishing

Impressum / Imprint

Bibliografische Information der Deutschen Nationalbibliothek: Die Deutsche Nationalbibliothek verzeichnet diese Publikation in der Deutschen Nationalbibliografie; detaillierte bibliografische Daten sind im Internet über http://dnb.d-nb.de abrufbar.
Alle in diesem Buch genannten Marken und Produktnamen unterliegen warenzeichen-, marken- oder patentrechtlichem Schutz bzw. sind Warenzeichen oder eingetragene Warenzeichen der jeweiligen Inhaber. Die Wiedergabe von Marken, Produktnamen, Gebrauchsnamen, Handelsnamen, Warenbezeichnungen u.s.w. in diesem Werk berechtigt auch ohne besondere Kennzeichnung nicht zu der Annahme, dass solche Namen im Sinne der Warenzeichen- und Markenschutzgesetzgebung als frei zu betrachten wären und daher von jedermann benutzt werden dürften.

Bibliographic information published by the Deutsche Nationalbibliothek: The Deutsche Nationalbibliothek lists this publication in the Deutsche Nationalbibliografie; detailed bibliographic data are available in the Internet at http://dnb.d-nb.de.
Any brand names and product names mentioned in this book are subject to trademark, brand or patent protection and are trademarks or registered trademarks of their respective holders. The use of brand names, product names, common names, trade names, product descriptions etc. even without a particular marking in this works is in no way to be construed to mean that such names may be regarded as unrestricted in respect of trademark and brand protection legislation and could thus be used by anyone.

Coverbild / Cover image: www.ingimage.com

Verlag / Publisher:
LAP LAMBERT Academic Publishing
ist ein Imprint der / is a trademark of
AV Akademikerverlag GmbH & Co. KG
Heinrich-Böcking-Str. 6-8, 66121 Saarbrücken, Deutschland / Germany
Email: info@lap-publishing.com

Herstellung: siehe letzte Seite /
Printed at: see last page
ISBN: 978-3-659-34040-6

DEDICATION

I would like to dedicate this work to my parents, my husband, my kids Yanis and Salma, my brothers and sisters as well as my in-laws.

ACKNOWLEDGEMENTS

Given that this work is based on my doctorate dissertation, I am deeply grateful to my supervisor, Prof. Yamina El Kirat, for her guidance, advice and constructive criticism without which the present study would not have been completed in its present form.

I would like to extend my gratitude to many members of the Ayt Merghad community who kindly accepted to participate in the study as interviewees.

I am also grateful to Reddad Erguig, Nourddine Amrous and Abdelmounim choqairi for having read the work. Their comments and suggestions were very useful.

It also gives me a great deal of pleasure to thank all the members of our research unit, be them teachers or fellow students. I have learnt a lot during our discussions and debates that took place during our regular meetings.

My deepest appreciation goes to all my family members, whose encouragement and help throughout my academic life have been of great value. Last but not least, I wish to warmly thank my husband, Hssein, whose continuous support and patience were invaluable.

TABLE OF CONTENTS

Page

DEDICATION i
ACKNOWLEDGEMENTS ii
TABLE OF CONTENTS iii
PHONETIC TRANSCRIPTION... iv
LIST OF PHOTOS... v
LIST OF MAPS vi
LIST OF TABLES vii
LIST OF FIGURES... viii
INTRODUCTION... 1
....PART ONE: THE AYT MERGHAD AREA AND COMMUNITY
.... 9
   The Origin of Ayt Merghad 10
   The Ayt Merghad Community: A Historical Overview....................................... 12
   The Socio-economic Transformations in The Ayt Merghad Area..................... 20
   Urbanization of the Ayt Merghad area... 26
   Immigration in the Ayt Merghad area.. 28
   Conclusion.. 31
.... PART TWO: BIRTH RITUALS AMONG AYT MERGHAD
.... 33
   The Traditional Birth Rituals among Ayt Merghad 34
     Pregnancy: Rites of Separation... 34
     The Post-delivery Stage: Rites of Transition 37
     The Celebration: Rites of Incorporation.. 44
.... PART THREE: DISCUSSION
.... 55
   Birth and The Evil Eye in The Ayt Merghad Culture 56
   Gender Preferences among Ayt Merghad 62
   The Loss of Birth Rites and Urbanization.. 68
CONCLUSION 85
BIBLIOGRAPHY 89

PHONETIC TRANSCRIPTION

The phonetic transcription adopted in the present study conforms to the International Phonetic Alphabet (IPA). Geminate sounds are indicated by means of doubling the consonant. For example:

Non-geminate	Geminate
m	mm
b	bb

Emphatic sounds are indicated by means of a letter with a dot underneath. For example:

Non-emphatic	Emphatic
d	ḍ
t	ṭ

LIST OF PHOTOS

Photo 1. The Zaabel Tunnel in 1930 ....*16*

Phtoto 2. Zaïd Ou Skounti: An Ayt Merghad Chief *17*

Photo 3. Assou Ou Basslam and the General Huré accept the pacification program *19*

Photo 4. An Ayt Merghad shepherdess in the 1940's *25*

Photo 5. taḥrujt and aṣamṭ used to wrap and swaddle a baby (2012) *38*

Photo 6. An Ayt Merghad baby's left hand with a bracelet made of black

beads, a Hamsa hand and a shell as a protection against the evil eye (2009)...........*42*

Photo 7. A necklace used as a protection against the evil eye (2012) *43*

Photo 8. An Ayt Merghad baby's legs adorned with henna with the left

one surrounded by an amulet (2009) *44*

Photo 9. Sheep is slaughtered on the seventh day (2008) *46*

Photo 10. A drawing that illustrates an Ayt Merghad woman with ixərban on her hair *48*

Photo 11. Some of the accessories used by an Ayt Merghad tamzurt *49*

Photo 12. An Ayt Merghad couple celebrating the birth of their male baby (2008) *50*

Photo 13. An Ayt Merghad father placing his baby on his mother's back (2008) *51*

Photo 14. An Ayt Meghad baby with the Quran next to its head (2009) *60*

Photo 15. Ibrahim Al Amrawi health centre in Tinjdad (2011) *76*

LIST OF MAPS

Map 1. The Confederacy of Ayt Yafelman *12*

Map 2. Gold trade route *14*

Map 3. Rural and urban areas in Errachidia (1997)..*27*

Map 4. The location of the fieldwork site *28*

LIST OF TABLES

Table 1. The Distribution of Ferkla Population in 2004 21

Table 2. The Schooling Rate by Level in Ferkla (2004) 22

Table 3. Poverty Rate in Ferkla 23

Table 4. Domestic Equipments in Ferkla 23

Table 5. Public sanitary establishments in Errachidia 75

LIST OF FIGURES

Figure 1. The Evolution of Ferkla Population between 1960 and 2004 ....*21*

Figure 2. Ferkla's Economic Characteristics *24*

Figure 3. Infant mortality rate in Morocco, 1976-2010

      (Infant deaths per 1000 live births) *75*

INTRODUCTION

During the last decades, Morocco has embarked on a proactive process of modernization and development. At the economic level, Morocco has instituted a series of development plans to modernize the economy and increase the production. However, the policy makers have disregarded the inherently close links that exist between culture and development. Adopting models of development that ignore and marginalize the multi-cultural aspect of the nation has led to the gradual loss of the country's cultural heritage. The current state of the Amazigh culture provides compelling evidence in that respect.

The present study seeks to provide an account of the impact of socio-economic development on the Amazigh cultural heritage in Morocco in general and among Ayt Merghad in particular. More specifically, the study is concerned with the investigation of the gradual loss of the Amazigh culture among Ayt Merghad, with a special focus on the birth rituals. It also tries to determine the factors behind the disappearance of most of the practices related to these rituals. From an ethnographic perspective (Boas, 1943; Blumer, 1969; Wilcox, 1982; Lincoln and Guba, 1985; LeCompte and Preissle, 1993; Woods, 1994; Gold, 1997; Massey 1998), the researcher tries to: (i) provide a thorough description of the birth rituals in the pre-independence era among Ayt Merghad, (ii) identify the major transformations these rituals have witnessed during the post-independence era and (iii) account for the impact of the socio-economic process of development in Morocco on the traditional birth rites among Ayt Merghad.

The state of birth rituals among Ayt Merghad stands witness to the transformations that the Amazigh culture among this tribal group has undergone. In order to understand the present-day birth-related practices, the researcher has set as a baseline of comparison a description of the traditional birth rites in the pre-independence era. On the basis of the information collected from old informants and different documents about both Ayt Merghad (Hart, 1978; Kastani, 2005 and Skounti, 1995) and the neighboring tribes like Ayt Atta (Hart, 1981, 1984), Ayt Hdiddou (Hart, 1978) and Ayt Khabbash (Becker, 2006), the researcher intends to reconstruct the birth rituals of the pre-independence era and take them as a point of departure for the exploration of the subsequent changes. The aim is to uncover the forces that have reshaped these practices and transformed them into their current state. A better understanding of the significance of these changes requires situating them in the context of the wider transformations experienced by the whole society as a result of the process of socio-economic development.

The main assumption underlying the present study is that development and urbanization in Morocco have had a great impact on the Moroccan society in general and the Amazigh community in particular. Culture, in general, is not considered a basic constituent in society, but rather a purely instrumental means to achieve economic progress (Skelton and Atten, 1999). The Amazigh creative traditions in Morocco are presented as folkloric, and, therefore, they have lost their real value as fundamental social constituents. Put differently, the Amazigh culture is not valued as a heritage, but it is a means to promote economic progress and tourism.

The researcher has chosen to focus on two main phases in the history of Morocco, namely the pre- and post-independence era. The choice of the period is grounded on the assumption that after the independence, Morocco has witnessed a number of mutations which have resulted in radical changes in the Moroccan culture in general and the Amazigh one in particular. Although Morocco was colonized for a relatively short period of time, 1912-1956, the effect of these decades on the Moroccan society and culture is immense. The entrance of the Europeans into Morocco has resulted in a change in the political, economic and social systems. The transformation and westernization of the political system was a major change introduced by the colonizer. Since independence, the centralization of authority in the hands of the government has been strengthened; and the power of the Amazigh tribal institutions has been shaken. For example, *ljma3t* and the customary law which constituted an

3

integral part of the Ayt Merghad system are no longer functional in the new political system.

At the economic level, the colonizers introduced new commercial methods and institutions which supplanted the traditional ones. Therefore, the banking system and industrialization have largely contributed to the development of big cities. This was mainly noticed in places like Casablanca and Rabat which attracted immigrants from rural areas. The latter escaped from drought and the deterioration of agriculture and sought cities to improve their living standards. This rural exodus permitted people to have contact with the culture of cities, a thing which affected their identity.

The introduction of the western technology and the French educational system has also resulted in radical permutations in the Moroccan culture and mentality. Before colonization, the educational system was based on Quranic schools. With the introduction of the French educational system, all school subjects, apart from Islamic studies, were taught in French. Thus, the language of the colonizer emerged as the language of science and modernity. This, in turn, had a significant impact on the Moroccan attitudes towards their native language and, by implication, their culture. Even after independence, Morocco inherited the French educational and administrative systems. Therefore, the prestige of the French language pushed Moroccans to invest on its mastery in order to be functional in the job market. The French educational system largely affected people's way of thinking, and some of them started adopting the Western values and life style at the expense of the traditional culture and mode of life. This is clearly shown in the following statement:

> *"Viewed in a historical perspective, the French occupation of Morocco and the subsequent establishment of a protectorate marked, on the one hand, the end of the traditional Moroccan culture which had survived since the introduction of Islam, and, on the other hand, the birth of "Neo-Moroccan culture" distinguished by a unique amalgamation of influences from the traditional past, from*

*recent developments in other Islam states, from French 20th
century culture, and what has sometimes been designated as
the "International Culture of the 20th century."* (Hoffman,
1967:172)

To fully examine the research questions, Van Gennep's model of rites of
passage was adopted. Van Gennep (1960) recognizes that all rites of passage,
including those marking birth, marriage, and death, share a common tripartite
structure. They are composed of rites of separation, rites of transition, and rites
of incorporation. Rites of separation remove a person from a previously
occupied state. Rites of transition, however, are performed when the person is
detached from the original state but not fully integrated in the new one. In the
final stage, rites of incorporation are carried out and are meant to integrate the
individual into a new state.

According to Van Gennep (1960), for a new self to exist, the old one must
ritually die. Candidates for some rites would be separated from the status to be
left behind, leaving familiar companions, the surroundings and the home. Second,
they enter a 'between' period, in which they become deprived of the
distinguishing marks of status and expressions of their old identity. Before
moving to the next stage, during segregation, the individual undergoes rituals
meant to deprive him of his identity and separate him from his previous social
status. He may move geographically or lose some physical markings of his
previous self. The individual has to acquire new skills and begin a reorientation
toward his future status. Only after this period of learning is complete, does the
person undergo the third phase of reincorporation into society. However, he does
so with his new status and identity, perhaps involving a new name or title, forms
of dress or style of language and, almost certainly, new patterns of behaviour
with appropriate duties and responsibilities.

Van Gennep (1960) views rites of passage as an essential ingredient in the
renovation of society. He believes that rites of passage serve to preserve social

stability by easing the transition of cohorts of individuals into a new status and prestigious roles. In the absence of rites of passage, society would be troubled with conflict as individuals either struggle to assert a new social status or deny a certain status. Van Gennep (1960) also explains the prevalence of rites of passage by noting their psychotherapeutic quality. Such rituals give individuals social support in confronting the anxiety they may feel facing new social roles or major life changes, such as parenthood or the death of loved ones. Fundamentally, Van Gennep (1960) argues that the function of this ritual framing of transitions is to restore equilibrium to the social order in the face of an ever-changing environment.

In order to meet the objectives of the study, an ethnographic approach is adopted. Two data collection techniques are used, namely participant observation and in-depth interviews. An overt approach to participation is adopted. As for the in-depth interviews, they are conducted in two different phases. The first phase involves informal conversational interviews with the informants selected through random sampling. During the second phase, key informants, who are famous in the community for being well-informed about the issues investigated, are targeted. This step is meant to involve the latter in the process of data analysis through checking the researcher's interpretations. The purpose of these second-phase-interviews is also to target specific questions and to deepen the researcher's understanding of the issues investigated.

It is worth mentioning that other sources of data are also used. Videos and photographs of ceremonies of birth were studied in the presence of some respondents who comment on them. Moreover, anthropological literature, though not directly related to Ayt Merghad, but to neighboring communities, helped gain an understanding of how lifecycle rituals were traditionally performed. Moreover, in order to understand the socio-economic mutations Morocco has witnessed since its independence and support the ethnographic data, the results of the national censuses and development indicators from the World Bank databases are consulted.

Thematically, the study is an ambitious contribution to the growing literature on the Amazigh culture. Being the first study of its kind to focus on the impact of socio-economic development on the birth rituals among Ayt Merghad, the book can be classified as an enriching study for several reasons. First, research on the topic in the south-eastern area of Morocco suffers from a dearth, and the focus of the available ethnographic studies has been mainly on a few tribes, namely Ayt Khabbash (Becker, 2006), Ayt Hdiddou (Hart, 1978) and Ayt Atta (Hart, 1981, 1984); Ayt Merghad, however, the target community, received little attention. Second, most of the studies about rituals in the south-eastern area of Morocco focused mainly on marriage ceremonies (Jlok, 1993); whereas birth, to the best of our knowledge, remain unexamined.Therefore, the present work differs and complements the existing studies by focussing on birth rituals at two main phases in the history of Morocco, namely the pre- and post-independence era. Third, birth-related practices, in this study, are not investigated in isolation; on the contrary, they are examined in relation to the process of socio-economic development Morocco has witnessed since its Independence.

PART ONE: THE AYT MERGHAD AREA AND COMMUNITY

The Origin of Ayt Merghad

In order to solve the mystery of the name Ayt Merghad, Skounti (1995) suggests an etymological analysis of the word. He states that the root of the word is trilateral √RΓD with the '*m*' being used in Amazigh to denote the agent. The root √RΓD is widespread in the Tamazight of central Morocco. It is used under the form '*rɣud*' which means 'to favor'. Skounti (1995), states that when the '*m*' of the agent is added to the word, it gives '*ameryud*' which seems to be singular, and '*imeryad*' is the plural form, on which the name Ayt Merghad is based.

Moreover, the origin of Ayt Merghad has been the subject matter of different studies, and different versions are available in the literature. According to Hart (1984), Ayt Merghad descended from the Portuguese. In the fourteenth and fifteenth centuries, the Portuguese occupied the Atantic coast of Morocco and they were combated by *mujahidin* 'fighters for Islam'. Hart (1984: 46) also claims that Ayt Merghad are referred to as *Ayt l-bultqiz*, a nickname used to refer to the Portuguese. He, therefore, states that:

> "*Any man-made or natural object which has a patently pre- or non-Islamic appearance tends to be shrugged off as "Portuguese". Hence it is an insult to refer to a tribe or a tribal segment as Ayt or ulad l-burtqiz, a term applied on occasion to the Ayt Murghad.*"

According to the legend, Ayt Merghad are descended from Dadda Merghad, who is Dadda Atta's brother. They are also named *Ayt iɣərm n'udi*, 'butter owners', because they used to give butter to Ayt Atta. One day, a member of Ayt Atta asked a woman from Ayt Merghad to give him some butter to rub it on his sandals. The woman refused; whereupon, the man picked up his sandals and slapped her on her face. Everyone in the region was informed about the incident. As a reaction, they decided to form *llef* 'confederacy' in order to take revenge against Ayt Atta (kastani, 2005; Hart, 1985 and Skounti, 1995).

This confederacy included different tribes. In addition to Ayt Merghad, the following tribes were part of it: Ayt Hdiddou, Ayt Izdig, Ayt Yahya, Ayt Aisa Bu Amar, and Ayt Mgild as Map 1. below illustrates. They all had an agreement drawn up to the effect that they would find peace by taking revenge against Ayt Atta. Thus the confederacy of Ayt Yafelman was formed, and Ayt Merghad were the leading force. The confederacy of Ayt Yafelman attacked Ayt Atta resulting in an endless hostility between the two groups.

Map 1. The Confederacy of Ayt Yafelman

Carte N° 2 : Le pays des Ayt Yafelmàn et ses abords à la fin du XIX° siècle.

Source: Peyron (1984: 128)

It is worth mentioning that the name *yafelman* is derived from the Amazigh phrase *afat alman*, meaning 'find peace'. Hart (1978:57) argues that because *"the Ait Medul, the children of Midul, constantly made war against their neighbors, their peace-loving mother finally cried 'afat alman! Afat alman! Find tranquility! Find peace!. And hence the name Ait Yafalman".*

The Ayt Merghad Community: A Historical Overview

A close look at the history of Ayt Merghad shows that the community inhabited one of the most important cities in Morocco, namely Sijilmassa. Since

12

the Middle Ages, the region has been called Tafilalet. The latter refers to the Southeast Morocco until the country's independence in 1956. After that, the region became known as Ksar Es-Souk Province which would later become Errachidia Province (Llahiane, 2004). Sijilmassa was founded in A.D. 757 by the Zennata Imazighen and flourished for 650 years. During the last two years of its existence, it was inhabited by approximately 30.000 people (Lightfoot & Miller, 1996).

Sijilmassa controlled the trans-Saharan gold trade and connected the Mediterranean and the Islamic world with West Africa. Merchants coming from different parts of the world followed the caravan trade route in the direction of Sijilmassa. Given its strategic position in the international trade,

> *"Sijilmassa quickly emerged as the premier desert entrepot of North Africa. Not only did the oasis secure the gold from south of the Sahara, it also controlled minting, sped the precious trade north and eastward, and was regarded by Arab geographers and historians as the wealthiest of the Maghrib."* (Lightfoot & Miller, 1996: 78)

Map 2. Gold trade route

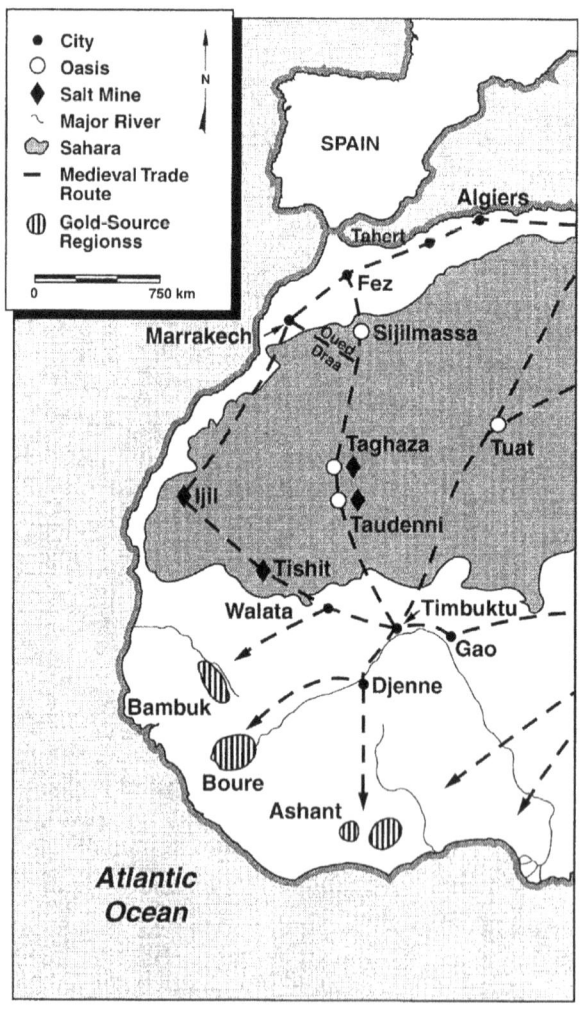

Source: Lightfoot & Miller (1996)

Sijilmassa managed to generate wealth and become the capital of the international trade. Because of its strategic position in the Maghreb and the high profit it made from commerce, Sijilmassa was targeted by many powers. Over the course of its history, which spanned from the mid 8th century until the end of

14

the 14th century, Sijilmassa fell under the control of many dynasties namely the Fatimids, the Almoravides, the Almohades, The Beni wattas, the Saadiyin, the Alawites. Apart from the Fatimides and the Alawites who are Arabs, the other dynasties originated among the Amazigh tribes. Kastani (2005) states that the Ayt Merghad tribe was one of the Sanhaja Amazigh tribes which united under the name of the Almoravides. The latter came with a new religious philosophy and demanded the spread of Islam. They brought their religious reform first to Sijilmassa before spreading it in the entire Maghreb. From the year 1053, the Almoravids began to spread Islam in the Amazigh areas of the Sahara, and to the regions south of the desert. After winning over the Sanhaja Amazigh tribe, they quickly took control of the entire desert trade route, seizing Sijilmassa in 1054. Following the Almoravides's paths, the other dynasties that ruled Sijilmassa had always taken the religious reform as a pretext in order to get control over the trade of gold and slaves. Llahian (2004: 43) argues that

> *"these dynasties had always rallied behind the religious agenda of purging Islam of its impurities to reach power; they all get to power in the name of the ideology if religious reforms. Their target however, was to control the masses and the luxurious caravan trade of gold and slaves."*

During the fifteenth and sixteenth centuries, Morocco suffered from famine and plagues. This negatively affected the Moroccan state control over the trade routes and monopoly of the trans-Sahara trade in favor of the Europeans. In the seventeenth and eighteenth centuries, the effect of drought, famine and the scarcity of resources were clear on the region of Tafilalet. This had created a strong competition over the resources among the various tribes. During the nineteenth century, battles over the palm groves reached its peak leading to the appearance of three main powers, namely, the Ayt Atta confederation to the west, the Dwi Mni3 to the east, and the Ayt Yaflman confederation, to which Ayt Merghad belong, to the north. In 1818, Sijilmassa was destroyed and Ayt

Atta got control over the palm groves and its hinterlands. The situation pushed Ayt Yaflman to react violently. Conflicts between the two confederations continued until the French put a military governorship in Tafilalet in 1930.

In order to get access to Tafilalet, the colonial forces dug the Zaabel tunnel in a mountain between Errich and Errachidia as shown in photo 1. This tunnel allowed the troops to achieve the target area.

Photo 1. The Zaabel Tunnel in 1930

Source : http://tribusdumaroc.free.fr/aityafelmane.php

However, getting control over the southeastern Morocco was not an easy undertaking. The French occupation of Tafilalet faced a strong resistance on the part of the Ayt Merghad community. This tribe reacted violently to the French occupation and showed a strong courage to defend their territory. Under the leadership of Zaïd Ou Skounti, Ali Ou Termoun, Moha Arji, among others, the Ayt Merghad community participated in various battles against the French colonial army. According to Skounty (n.d.), Zaïd Ou Skounti was one of the most influential figures in the resistance of the Southeast area.

Phtoto 2. Zaïd Ou Skounti: An Ayt Merghad Chief

Source: Skounti (n.d.)

Zaïd Ou Skounti participated in a number of battles against the colonial forces, namely:

- The Boudenib battle in 1908

- The Tafilalet battles in 1918-1919

- The Todgha battles in 1918-1919

- The Aït Yaâqoub and Tounfit battles in 1929-1930

- The Tadra battle in 1930

- The Tazegzaout battle in 1930

- The Serdar battle in 1930

To support their neighbouring Ayt Atta tribe, who waged a war against the colonial army in 1933, the Ayt Merghad tribe participated in the ferocious Jbel Saghro battle under the leadership of Assou Ou Basslam (khettouch n.d). The latter managed to defeat the French who soon after reacted violently.

Llahian (2004: 56) states that *"This Frernch loss was quickly reversed by the devastating French bombardment of ksars, tents, and herds."* Under the pressure of protecting the area from more damage, the Ayt Atta submitted to the French pacification program on condition not to be ruled and taxed by the Pasha El Glaoui.

Photo 3. Assou Ou Basslam and the General Huré accept the pacification program

The battle of Jbel Badou carried out by Ayt Merghad is another key event in the history of this tribe's resistance. The battle was a major contribution to the end of the French colonialism. In 1933, the Ayt Merghad tribe, under the leadership of Zaid Ou Skounty decided to lead an organized armed struggle in order to put an end to the French penetration in the southeast Morocco. In fact, not only men took part in these battles. Women too participated and took care of the veterans. Eluizi (2010) argues that

"… toute une population avait été mobilisée dans ces batailles. Les femmes n'étaient jamais loin des champs de combattants par des "warru" (chants berbères) et entachaient les déserteurs par du henné, une manière d'en faire la risette de la communauté."

"… all the population was mobilized in these battles. Women were never away from the battle fields. They took care of the injured, encouraged the warriors by chanting "warru" (Amazigh songs) and stained the deserters with henna, as a way to be laughted at by the community members."

In 29 August 1933, Zaid Ou Skounty inflicted a historic defeat on the colonial soldiers who were led by the General Huré.

However, the Ayt Merghad community paid too high for their heroic resistance. In an attempt to protect their territory from the colonial forces, the Ayt Merghad farming system and irrigation infrastructure had been immensely affected. The French bombardment of the *ksours* "villages" and fields caused a lot of damage to the area, a matter which led to the scarcity of resources in the region.

The Socio-economic Transformations in The Ayt Merghad Area

Recently, the Ayt Merghad area in general and Ferkla in particular has undergone some socio-economic mutations. Today, the inhabitants of Ferkla benefit from a number of services and infrastructure (e.g. paved roads, electricity, drinking water, schools, hospitals, administrative services and an extensive telephone network), which was not the case a few decades ago. Road connections and transport facilities to destinations outside Ferkla have also improved during the last five decades.

According to the most recent population census, Morocco's population has grown from slightly less than 11 millions inhabitants in 1960 to 29.9 millions in

2004. This growth has been mostly apparent in urban areas. In the context of Ferkla, the population has grown from 19142 in 1960 to 22086 in 1971 and then to 29916 in 1982. In 1994, the population reached 37297 and according to the results of the last census of 2004 it has doubled since the 60's and has reached 40266 in 2004 (RGPH, 1960, 1971, 1982, 1994, 2004). The following figure illustrates the evolution of Ferkla population between 1960 and 2004.

Figure 1. The Evolution of Ferkla Population between 1960 and 2004

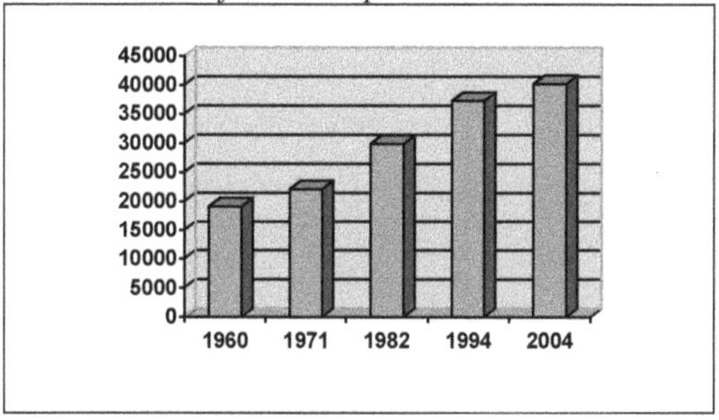

Source: HCP – RGPH, 1960, 1971, 1982, 1994, 2004

Concerning the distribution of the population of Ferkla, 82% of the whole population lives in the rural areas. Only 18% live in Tinjdad, which is considered an urban area. Around half (50.1%) of the inhabitants lives in Ferkla Al Oulia. As for Ferkla Assoufla, it is inhabited by 31.3% of the population. For ease of reference, the following table illustrates the distribution of Ferkla's population.

Table 1. The Distribution of Ferkla Population in 2004

	Ferkla Polulation								
	Tinjdad (urban)			Ferkla al Oulia (rural)			Ferkla Assoufla (rural)		
	male	female	total	male	female	total	male	female	total
	3553	3928	7481	9604	10562	20166	5890	6729	12619
	47.5%	52.5%	18.5%	47.6%	52.4%	50.1%	46.7%	53.3%	31.3%
Total	40266								

Source: HCP – RGPH, 2004

At the educational level, the Ministry of National Education was created in 1959. Then, compulsory education was introduced in the early 1960s. At that stage, the enrollments of school-age children was 60.3% at the level of Ferkla (RGPH, 1960, 2004). The highest enrollment rates are noticed at the primary level, with 44.3% in Tinjdad, 56.3% in Ferkla al Oulia and 66.3% in Ferkla Assoufla. However, these rates decrease as students move upwards within the educational system to reach 10.9% in Tinjdad in 6% in Ferkla al Oulia and 3.5% in Ferkla Assoufla at the university level. It is also noticed that these numbers are heavily in favor of the male population and urban areas (RGPH, 2004). The following table provides detailed statistics of the schooling rate at different levels in Ferkla.

Table 2. The Schooling Rate by Level in Ferkla (2004)

	Schooling rate in Ferkla								
	Tinjdad population 7481			Ferkla al Oulia population 20166			Ferkla Assoufla population 12619		
	Male	female	total	male	female	total	male	female	total
Preschool Quranic	175 (3.4%)	134 (2.6%)	309 (6%)	238 (2.2%)	187 (1.6%)	425 (3.8%)	199 (2.7%)	21 (0.3%)	220 (3%)
Primary	1150 (22.2%)	1141 (22.1%)	2291 (44.3%)	3489 (29.4%)	3182 (26.9%)	6671 (56.3%)	2411 (33.1 %)	2413 (33.2%)	4824 (66.3%)
Junior High School	600 (11.6%)	652 (12.6%)	1252 (24.2%)	1618 (13.7%)	1271 (10.7%)	2889 (24.4%)	1045 (14.3 %)	573 (7.9%)	1618 (22.2%)
High School	490 (9.5%)	264 (5.1%)	754 (14.6%)	787 (6.6%)	330 (2.8%)	1117 (9.4%)	294 (4%)	66 (0.9%)	360 (4.9%)
University	395 (7.6%)	169 (3.3%)	564 (10.9%)	559 (4.7%)	152 (1.3%)	711 (6%)	238 (3.3%)	16 (0.2%)	254 (3.5%)

Source: HCP – RGPH, 2004

The area also records a relatively high percentage of families living under the poverty line. The results of the 2004 census show that 31.6% of the households in Ferkla suffer from poverty, which reveals the difficult living conditions in the region (RGPH, 2004). The severity of poverty is mainly apparent in rural areas, namely Ferkla al Oulia 47.3% and Ferkla Assoufla

33.1%. However, only 14.5% of the households in Tinjdad, which is an urban area, are living under the poverty line. The following table illustrates the rate of poverty in Ferkla.

Table 3. Poverty Rate in Ferkla

	Number of households	households living under the poverty line	Poverty Rate
Tinjdad	1289	187	14.5%
Ferkla Al Oulia	3010	1424	47.3%
Ferkla Assoufla	1713	567	33.1%

Source: HCP – RGPH, 2004

Notwithstanding, the area is characterized by a good access to communication devices. The area has high rates of connections to electricity and drinking water. The results of the 2004 census show that 85.6% of the houses in Ferkla are equipped with electricity and 54.1% benefit from the drinking water. Concerning domestic equipments, 85.6 % of the houses own a television, and 52% have a satellite dish. 11.3% of the houses possess land phone and 69.9% have at least one cellular phone (RGPH, 2004). More detailed statistics about the different communes in Ferkla are presented in the following table.

Table 4. Domestic Equipments in Ferkla

Place	Number of Houses	Communication devices				Drinking Water	Electricity
		TV	Satellite Dish	Land Phone	cellular Phone		
Tinjdad	1289	1164 (90.3%)	865 (67.1%)	202 (15.7%)	1009 (78.3%)	1181 (91.6%)	1180 (91.5%)
Ferkla al Oulia	3010	2392 (79.5%)	1390 (46.2%)	314 (10.4%)	1980 (65.8%)	2115 (70.3%)	2311 (76.8%)
Ferkla Assoufla	1713	1493 (87.2%)	731 (42.7%)	137 (8%)	1126 (65.7%)	9 (0.5%)	1517 (88.6%)
Total	6009	85.6%	52%	11.3%	69.9%	54.1%	85.6%

Source: HCP – RGPH, 2004

According to the 2004 census, 36.7 % of the total active population in Ferkla works in the agricultural sector. However, the sectors of public work, commerce, industry, and administration also employ a good part of the population. 41.1 % of the population is engaged in public work. 9.3% is working in the field of industry. 5.7% is working in commerce. 3.4% constitutes members of administrations. 3.8% of the population is engaged in other different activities (RGPH, 2004). In spite of the succession of years of dryness, the urbanization process and the appearance of new economic activities in the Ayt Merghad area, the population engaged in the agriculture is still high compared to other sectors. The following figure illustrates the economic characteristics of Ferkla.

Figure 2. Ferkla's Economic Characteristics

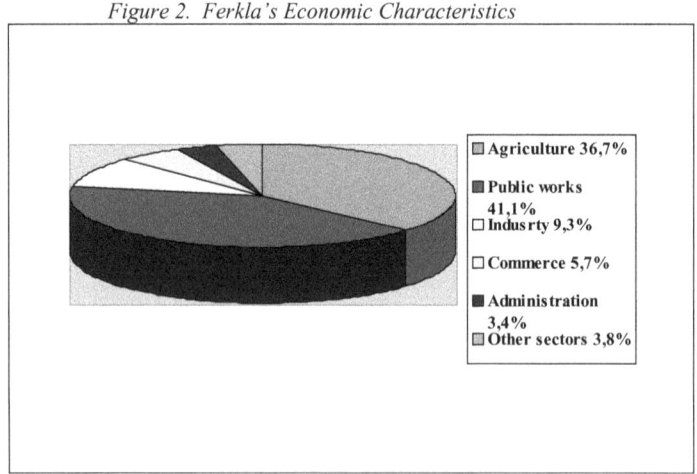

Source: HCP – RGPH, 2004

Population growth, urbanization, the decrease of illiteracy, relatively high levels of poverty and the diversification of the economic activities have marked the process of socioeconomic development during the last decades in Ferkla.

Photo 4. An Ayt Merghad shepherdess in the 1940's

Source: Robichez (1946)

Certainly, other resources contribute to the local development of the area. The role of the associations in the development of the Ayt Merghad area is not to be underestimated. Through an increasingly active associative movement, several projects are led at the local level and are supported by the State or the international agencies. For example, projects of the construction of roads and bridges, installation and management of generators, drinking water supply, literacy programs and campaigns against the endemic diseases are all parts of the associations' agendas. For exemple, 'Association Voix de la Jeunesse

Ferkla', 'Association Horizon pour la Culture et le Développement El Khorbat', 'Association el khorbat pour le Patrimoine et le Dévelopment' and 'Association Oasis Ferkla pour l'Environnement et le Patrimoine' are very active associations in Ferkla which contribute to the development of the area. New activities, in particular tourism, constitute an essential resource. Finally, the contributions of national or international emigration have played a considerable role in the socio-economic transformation of Ayt Merghad.

Urbanization of the Ayt Merghad area

As a result of the accelerated process of urbanization in Morocco, the urban population grew by 153% between 1960 and 1982 (Belghazi & Baden, 2002). The results of the general censuses of 1960, 1971, 1982, 1994 and 2004 are also very indicative of the sharp increase in the urbanization of Errachidia. The urbanization rate increased from 5.6% in 1960 to 9.25% in 1971. The census of 1982 indicates that the population of the province was 422.869; 82% of which were rural and 18% urban. Another increase in the urbanization rate is indicted by the 1994 census results, which show that the population of the province became 522.117, 25.75% of which were urban and 70.25% rural. More recent statistics show that the population of the province reached 556.612 with 64.88 % living in the rural area and 35.12 % in the urban one in 2004. It is worth mentioning that the urbanization rate has doubled between the seventies and the eighties. This can be attributed to the severe drought the area had known between 1979 and 1986; the fact that had triggered rural exodus. The high increase in the urban population is also attributed to the high rate of the population growth, the improvement of the standards of living in the urban areas and the availability of jobs (Alpert, 2007).

Map 3. Rural and urban areas in Errachidia (1997)

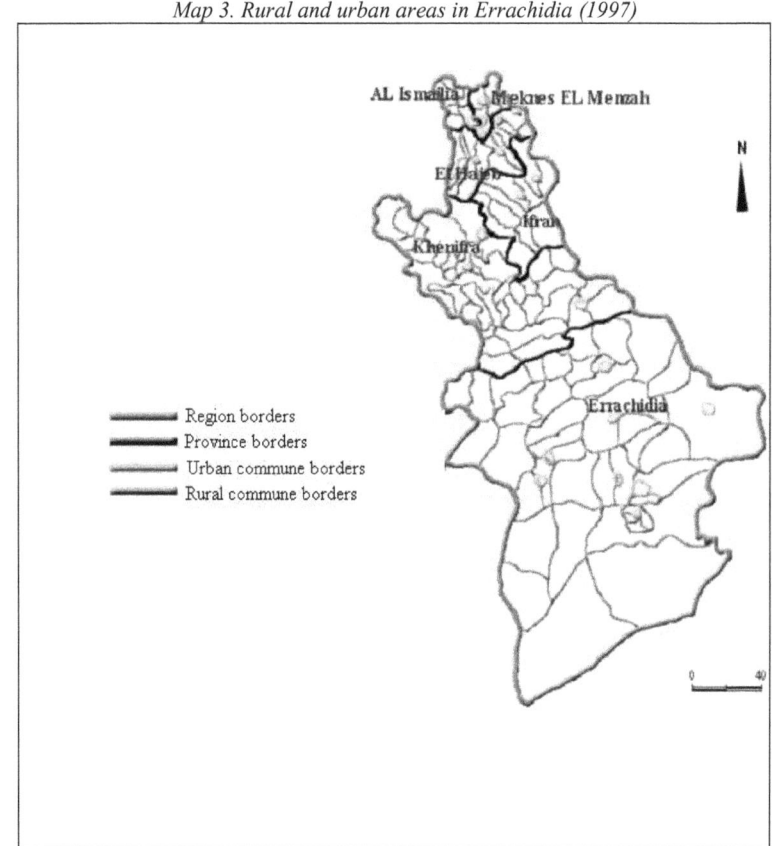

Source: HCP

The province of Errachidia belongs to the region of Meknes-Tafilalt. It consists of 44 communes, among which Ferkla, the area where the data of the present study were collected. Ferkla is inhabited by different ethnic groups namely, Ayt Merghad, the target group, Ayt Atta, Imazighn, Chourfa, Ikbleïn, Igouramne, and Ayt Bâali ou Ahmed. The area is organized into three main communes. Each one is subdivided into a number of *iyerman* (*ksour* in Arabic).

1- The Commune of Ferkla El Oulia : Ayt Assem, Ksours Sat, Khorbat, Azag Nouchen, Ksours Asrir, Nimro, Tamerdoult, Amellal, Tarouchte.

2- Municipality of Tinjdad: Ayt Mâamar, Tighdouine, Gardmeit, Tinjdad centre.

3- Commune of Ferkla El Soufla: Talalt, Tayrza, Tighfert, Ayt Ben Omar, Izelf, Ayt My El Mamoun, Tizgaghine, Lakssiba, Ktâa El Oued.

Map 4. The location of the fieldwork site

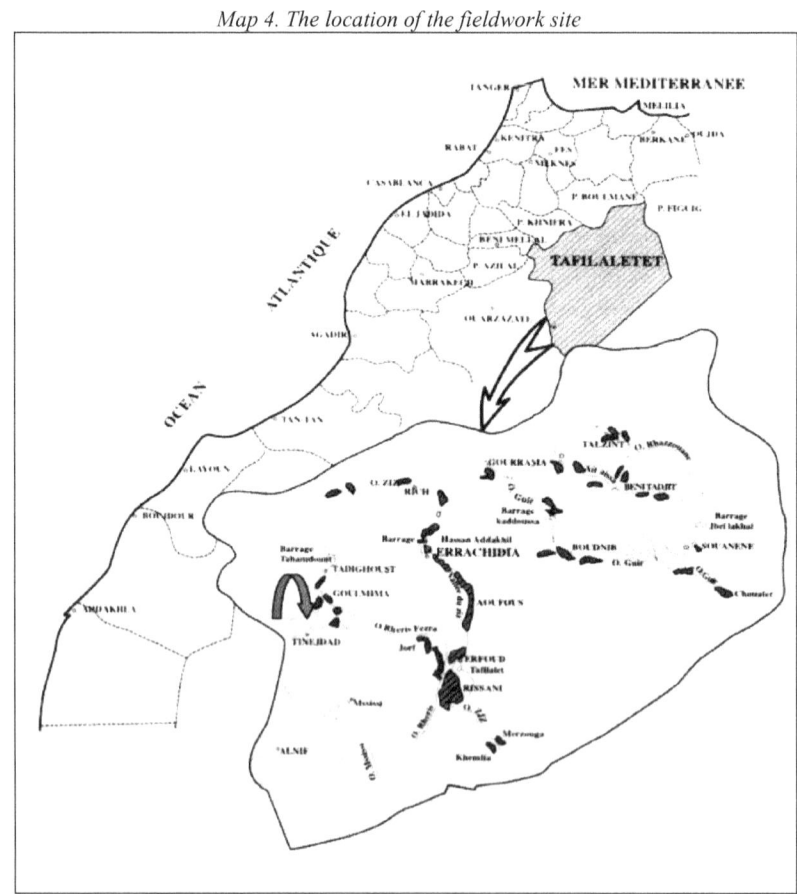

Source: adapted from Kabiri (n.d.)

Immigration in the Ayt Merghad area

Rural areas in Morocco are generally characterized by mass migration to the urban centers in the country and Europe. According to Bencherifa (1991), migration reaches its peak in regions that are affected by hard ecological conditions such as aridity. This is the case for the Ayt Merghad area. The hard and severe conditions in the region, the strong population growth and the effect of the repetitive periods of drought on agriculture forced many Ayt Merghad people to leave their villages and seek refuge mainly in big cities or in European industrial countries. The only exit out of this crisis appeared in the search for non-agricultural activities through emigration which constitutes a vital development resource that alleviates poverty and unemployment.

Following the example of other areas in Morocco, exodus towards the cities in the inner part of the country was considered by many Ayt Merghad. The urban areas, mainly Rabat and Casablanca, equipped with hospitals, schools, electricity, and drinking water constitute an ideal place for those seeking a comfortable standard of life compared with the difficult conditions in the rural areas.

For others, however, external emigration was a better choice. Berriane et. al. (2010: 35) claims that the southern area of Morocco *"was always classified as the third hearth of international emigration after Souss and Eastern Rif"*. In line with this claim, De Haas (2007), states that in several communities in Morocco's southern areas, between one fifth and half of all households have at least one member who has migrated abroad.

A number of factors have activated the process of migration in The Ayt Merghad area. The French colonization of Algeria marked the beginning of economic and political restructuring in that country, which created new job opportunities that in turn triggered the migration process in Morocco in general and in the Ayt Merghad area in particular. The increasing demand for manpower in the Algerian farms attracted a rising number of seasonal migrants from the southeastern Morocco. The colonial era in Morocco (1912 to 1956) also marked the beginning of migration to France. A need for manpower in France led to the recruitment of tens of thousands of Moroccans in factories, mines, and the French army (De Haas, 2005).

Actually, the wave of migration was weak during the pre-independence era compared to its state after independence. Emigration from the Ayt Merghad area reached its peak during the period between 1960 and 1974. This was mainly attributed to the severe drought the area witnessed during this period. Moreover, the economic progress that characterized European countries in the 1960s resulted in an increased demand for manpower. As a consequence, Morocco signed a number of labor-recruitment agreements with various European countries, namely, the former West Germany and France in (1963), Belgium in (1964), and the Netherlands in (1969) (De Haas, 2005). This led to diversity in the emigrants' destinations, which were initially limited to Algeria and France. Recently, Spain and Italy have also been targeted.

The emigration process has been encouraged by the Moroccan government for both political and economic reasons. As such, certain groups in some regions were encouraged to leave their home towns and villages in order to improve their social status and, ultimately, guarantee their loyalty. In this regard, De Haas (2005) argues that:

> "Ever since the 1960s, the Moroccan government has encouraged emigration on political and economic grounds. It stimulated labor recruitment from relatively marginal Berber-speaking areas of the southwestern Sous valley, the oases of southeastern Morocco, and the northern Rif Mountains, a region notorious for its rebellious attitude to central authority. In particular, remittances were expected to make a contribution to prosperity and thus dampen the rebellious tendency."

Economically speaking, the Ayt Merghad area has benefited a lot from the migrants' incomes. At the national level, the officially registered remittances increased from $23 million to $2.1 billion per year between 1968 and 1992 (De Haas, 2005). These incomes have contributed to the improvement of living conditions in Ferkla. The number of families living under the poverty line has recently declined, which has made people's purchase power higher. Therefore, farmers started using machines and technological tools in agriculture. Electricity and drinking water have also reached different rural areas.

However, emigration has strongly contributed to the cultural transformations the Ayt Merghad area has witnessed during the last five decades. Rural exodus and emigration abroad have largely influenced different aspects of life in Ferkla. These changes show in the disappearance of various customs and traditions and the adoption of new ones. The young generation has replaced traditional values and practices by others borrowed from either the urban areas or foreign countries. That is why De Mas (n.d.) has gone to the extent of stating that:

> *"When you look at lifestyle, the migrant regions have undergone a complete transformation in the last forty years. Morocco has been bombarded by external ideas, norms and values. For example on the age of marriage, on sex, but also on democracy, consumption levels, music. It is impossible to separate the increasing fundamentalism or conservatism from the enormous financial, moral and psychological influence from the West."*

Conclusion

A profound reflection on the past of the Ayt Merghad tribe makes it easy to note the community's excellence in many fields. From an economic perspective, Ayt Merghad were active participants on the economic front as they inhabited Sijilmassa. The era was a source of wealth for numerous other nations while its merchandise assured it penetration into many foreign markets.

A close look at the history of Morocco offers evidence for the heroic participation of the community in the war against colonization. This tribe reacted violently to the French occupation and showed a strong courage to defend their territory. Under the leadership of influential figures, the Ayt Merghad community participated in various battles against the French army and managed to inflict historic defeats on the colonial soldiers. Their role in the resistance against colonization was a major contribution to the end of the French penetration in the southeast Morocco.

At the level of the community's socio-political organization, segmentation, *ljma3t* and the customary law constitute an integral part of the Ayt Merghad system. Socially speaking, seven distinct traditional units are distinguished. These units are based upon blood relationship in the male line, decent from a common legendary ancestor and the geographical proximity. Politically, *ljma3t* is concerned with the maintenance of equilibrium in the tribe. Disputes between the community members are settled through reference to the customary law.

Recently, the Ayt Merghad area has undergone some socio-economic mutations. Today, the community members benefit from a number of services and infrastructure which was not the case a few decades ago. Road connections and transport facilities to destinations outside the area have improved during the last five decades. The area is also characterized by a good access to communication devices. Urbanization, immigration, the decrease of illiteracy, and the diversification of the economic activities are all prominent aspects that have marked the process of socio-economic development in the Ayt Merghad area.

PART TWO: BIRTH RITUALS AMONG AYT MERGHAD

The life-cycle rituals mark major transitions in the life of the individual. In the Ayt Merghad area, special rites surround birth. When a woman becomes a mother, she undergoes a social status change. The latter is accompanied by a number of rituals which serve to support her physically and emotionally after delivery and help her reintegrate into society. In this part, focus is on the various birth-related rituals, ranging from rites of pregnancy to rites observed at the actual time of childbirth and during the naming ceremony.

The Traditional Birth Rituals among Ayt Merghad

Pregnancy: Rites of Separation

The birth rituals, among Ayt Merghad, start with pregnancy. The latter is characterized by the performance of various rites of separation. An expectant mother used to apprehend the death of her newborn child; therefore, pregnancy used to be a state which was governed by a lot of anxiety. The death of a child in infancy was far more common than it is today. Given the high risk of birth complications and infant as well as maternal death, it is not surprising that pregnancy be surrounded by superstitions.

During the first stages of pregnancy, many safety measures are taken. It was widely believed that a pregnant woman is very vulnerable to risks. Women have to try hard to keep their pregnancy as a secret in order to avoid the evil eye. They should also be ashamed of announcing such news to the family members because pregnancy is a sign of sexual activity. Moreover, any sign of craving for specific types of food should be ignored. The pregnant woman has to eat from what all the family members eat and she does not have the right to prepare anything different for herself. In case she loses her appetite and cannot eat from what is available, she stays hungry.

A pregnant woman also has to do her best to avoid practices assumed to harm the baby. It is believed that funerals are a source of threat for a pregnant woman. The sad atmosphere accompanying death is assumed to be capable of harming and causing sickness to the baby. Therefore, a pregnant woman should not attend funerals as explained by a 54-year-old woman:

> *"llant wahli n lumur nna ixssa ad ur tg tməṭṭut iṭṭarun*
> *afad ṭhama iɣfəns d ujnna illan g udis nəs. g lmital, ixssa*
> *ad ur tḥiḍər i id l3zat xəṣ mç tti nmala bəzzaf wənna*
> *immutən. da ttinin aḥiḍər g id l3zat daj itḍurru bnadm.*
> *juwt tikəlt, iḍras bnadm i jllis n 3mmi dart ujnna t3zza*
> *tadʒart nəs nna mi jmmut urgaz."*

> *"There are many things which a pregnant woman should*
> *avoid in order to protect herself and her foetus. For*
> *example, she should not attend funerals unless the*
> *deceased is a relative. It is believed that attending*
> *funerals harms the baby. Once, my cousin miscarried*
> *after condoling her neighbour who lost her husband."*

In addition to that, the expectant mother has to avoid staring at someone who is handicapped or has any physical defect. It is believed that if her attention is attracted by someone with a specific abnormality, the latter might be transmitted to her baby. Thus, in case she finds herself in such a situation, the solution is to immediately spit. This practice is explained in the following quote made by A 62-year-old woman:

> *"ixssa adur tsçsiw tməṭṭut iṭṭarun g bnadm ifan ça aʃku*
> *iɣi ad izri ujnnaɣ s bnadm illan g udis nəs. mç djuwji*
> *rabbi tqqar diçs, ixssa at tslutf. ajnny ur inni ad ad jadʒ*
> *iɣn ça ad izri s bnadm nəs."*

> *"A pregnant woman should avoid looking at an*
> *abnormal person because this abnormality could be*
> *transmitted to her foetus. In case, she found herself*
> *staring at such a person, she should spit. This act will*
> *prevent the transmission of such a sickness to her*
> *foetus."*

To guarantee a safe delivery, other precautions are taken. It is believed that drawing attention to the baby brings bad luck to the latter. Therefore, parents did not use to prepare things for the baby or suggest a name until it was born. The usual reason given for this custom is pure superstition as stated by a 58-year-old woman *"ur iħli at ӡӡuӡt ça n lħwajӡ qbəl ad ilula bnadm, am uxtar n jism nɣd aӡӡuӡd n i3ban."* *"It is not good to prepare certain things for the coming baby. These include choosing a name or bringing clothes."*

In addition to that, women used to wear large clothes so as to hide their pregnancy and protect themselves from the evil eye. They are also expected to continue to perform work until the onset of labor, since hard work supposedly helps get an easier delivery. In this regard, an 84-year-old woman states that:

> *"tiwtmin zman daxddəmnt aṛ 3la ħal ad arunt. arasənt issuhan ujinnaɣ tarwa. am nkkin, ass nag riɣ ad aruɣ, zzrix tin g uzddam. ɣir gulaɣd taddart, jamzij uzbar, sa3tajn dart ujinnaɣ aruɣ."*

> *"Pregnant women used to work until the last minute before delivery. This was very beneficial for them as hard work would make the delivery an easy undertaking. In my case, for example, I spent the last day of my first pregnancy collecting wood in the field. Upon my arrival home, I felt the first signs of labor, and two hours later, the baby was born."*

Another 71-year-old woman claims that:

> *"datɣima tməṭṭut tarun g bərra, g igran nɣəd amərdul. da ttasij islli təbbij zars aṣərm tut tamurçist. tasid tasəlmja nəs. ur təlli tanna çi nnan had qad aruɣ qqimɣ. da xddəmnt ar das təddu tziri.*

> *"Sometimes, a woman would give birth outside the house, in the fields or at the desert. She would take a stone and use it to cut the umbilical cord, tie a knot, and take her baby back home. No woman would think of staying home as she might give birth at any time. Women used to work until they went into labor."*

The Post-delivery Stage: Rites of Transition

The post-delivery stage during the pre-independence era was also characterized by the performance of a number of rites. It was customary for the pregnant woman, in case she was living in a separate house, to go to her family-in-law's place of residence several days before the delivery's expected time. Childbirth used to take place at home and in secret. The process was considered strictly a female domain and men were forbidden from attending.

With the first signs of *tiziri* 'labor', the mother-in-law or any woman who has already given birth is called in order to assist in the birthing process. However, the presence of a birth attendant is not compulsory; the help of an experienced woman is sought only in complicated deliveries. Before the woman goes into labor, she prepares a number of items, namely, a sharp knife, razor or scissors, *tinsrit* 'a wool thread', *aṣamṭ* 'swaddling band made of wool', *taḥrujt* 'an old piece of cloth made of wool' , henna, a rope and some soil.

To relieve the birthing woman from discomfort and speed up the delivery, the birth attendant offers her some hot drinks such as soup and herbal tea. The woman in labor is also encouraged to move around and avoid lying down positions. To prepare the setting for the delivery, the birth attendant covers the area where the process will take place with some soil in order to protect the area form getting dirty, then she hangs a rope to the beams of the roof where the pregnant woman can pull herself up while giving birth. When the woman in labor feels that the contractions become stronger and once her water breaks, she squats while grasping the rope for support, then follows the urge to push. The birth attendant helps the birthing mother by holding her from the back. This state is illustrated in the following quote articulated by an 81-year-old woman.

> *"taddart ag urux rbə3ṭaʃ n warraw. dattili tagust g ugadir,ar digs n ttagl agatu. luqt nna d idda wʒbar i tməṭṭut, da tʒəbd s agatu, tkkast tməṭṭut dart ar ttarw. dilliy ur illa sbitar."*

"I gave birth to fourteen children at home. We used to hang a rope to the beams of the roof. When a woman went into labor, she would hold that rope, and another woman would help her from the back until she delivered. At that time, there was no hospital."

After the baby's birth, the attendant cuts the umbilical cord with a non-sterilized sharp knife, razor or scissors and ties it with *tinsrit* 'a wool thread'. This is usually done without taking any hygienic action such as washing the hands or cleaning the setting. The newborn is covered with dry henna which is removed soon after. The baby is then wrapped in *taḥrujt* 'an old piece of cloth made of wool' and swaddled from shoulders to feet using *aṣamṭ* 'swaddling band made of wool'. The newborn's head is very well tightened with *taçənbuft* 'a small scarf' assuming that this will prevent the baby from having a large head. The baby's eyes are also bordered with kohl as a way of protection.

Photo 5. taḥrujt and aṣamṭ used to wrap and swaddle a baby (2012)

After finishing with the baby, the birth attendant controls the mother until *timattin* 'the placenta' is delivered. Then, the placental ritual is immediately performed. The placenta is of great importance for Ayt Merghad because it is considered the baby's twin. Therefore, it is customary to carefully bury it in a secret place. In case the newborn is a girl, the placenta burial is performed on the same day, but if the baby is a boy; the placenta is kept next to the mother in order to keep an eye on it for the first three days. The community members believe that in case the placenta is found by someone, it could be used to harm the mother and the baby through magical practices. This state is manifested in the following quotes. A 74-year-old woman confesses that:

> *"ixssa atssufɣd timattin n tərbat fisa3,tadʒd tin ishirri. gʷwt lʒiht, da tsbajjant lm3azza d lfarħa n ishirri. g lʒiht jaḍn, ad ur ittug gifs ça."*

> *"You should get rid of a female baby's placenta as soon as possible, and keep that of a male baby. First, this is a sign of love and happiness for the birth of a male baby. Second, this is done out of fear that it might be used to harm the baby through magic."*

Another 67-year-old woman admits that:

> *"zman, ur da tssufuɣ taməṭṭut jurun l3il timattin afd ad ttarw ishirran. məç turw tamṭṭut l3il, dasənt iqqaz ça axjuj j lɣbar j təħuna idlasənt. mçəd tarbat, datnti tssufuɣ taddaɣ nnam ibbin tawitənt ar çan dinna g urak illa awd jan təɣzasənt tadrasənt."*

> *"In the past, a woman who gave birth to a male baby would not dispose of the placenta outside the home in order to keep giving birth to males. In the case of a male's birth, the placenta is buried in the stable of the house. When a female baby was born, the birth attendant would burry it in a deserted place."*

Before leaving, the birth attendant takes more care of the new mother. She offers the latter some melted butter. The new mother first rinses her mouth three times and pours the remaining butter in a bottle to reuse it to massage her nipples and her face in order to remove the pregnancy mask. Then, she drinks some of it. The new mother is also offered some *ṭ3am* 'home made pasta' mixed with butter to eat after breastfeeding her baby.

A rite that is performed by Ayt Merghad immediately after birth is whispering Islamic statements in the baby's ear. Most of the respondents state that the first words a newborn should hear are the words of Islam. A 52-year-old woman argues that:

> *"lħaӡa tamzwarut nna mi jxssa ad as tislli tsəlmja hija awal n rəbbi afad ad itdijjən inçər ig bu ddin, idfur abrid n rəbbi ur idfur çan ddin jaḍḍn. hat da tinin mdən nwid ajddy da is3raq tiṭ ula daj ttadӡa ʃʃiṭan ad inmili taslmja."*

> *"The first thing a baby should hear is God's words in order to be religious and, therefore, grow up following God's path without converting into another religion. Moreover, people say that this act is going to protect the baby from the evil eye and will not let Satan approach him."*

Therefore, the father or an old person whispers the *adan* 'call to prayers' in the right ear of the baby, and *iqama* 'the second call to prayers' in the left ear. Some respondents mention whispering just *ʃahada* 'the testimony of faith indicating belief in one God and that the prophet Mohammed "peace be upon him" is his prophet'. Others state that only *adan* is uttered. Although there is some controversy among the respondents concerning the statements to be said, all of them agree on the fact that words symbolizing Islam should be the first to be heard by a baby. The respondents also state that this rite is exclusively performed by males. Priority is given to the baby's father, but in his absence or in the presence of an older uncle that honor is given to the latter because *"çu jtxitir bnadm çu jtzajad g lʔiman çu jtzajad g tӡallit." "the older a person is the bigger his faith becomes. An old person also takes his prayers more seriously."* as stated by a 63-year-old man. Also, someone who has been to pilgrimage or an imam is a better qualified candidate to carry out the whispering action. Although this rite has its origins in Islamic laws, Ayt Merghad perform it as a practice among a series of precautionary measures. They believe that uttering the aforementioned statements will protect the baby from Satan, the Jinn and the evil eye.

After birth, the mother and the newborn enter a transition stage which is assumed to be surrounded by many dangers. They are considered vulnerable to attacks from the evil eye and the Jinn during the initial period after birth, which lasts up to forty days. *tiṭ* "the evil eye" is considered dangerous because it entails strong jealousy and envy towards the addressee. Ayt Merghad believe that the evil eye cannot only harm but also cause death. Therefore, it is highly feared and many precautionary measures are taken.

Once the relatives and neighbours are informed, they visit the new mother. In case the newborn is a boy, the family offers the guests *ḥluẓ* 'uncooked grinded wheat mixed with melted butter' as a symbol of prosperity and fertility. The news of a girl's birth, however, is not as significant as that of a boy. When a boy is born more precautions are taken to avoid the evil eye. On the announcement of the news of the latter's birth, the statement *llah ibarç* 'May God bless him' ought to be pronounced which is not the case in the birth of a female baby. The assumption underlying such a behavior is that girls are not that valuable, hence they will not be attacked by the evil eye. Thus, there is no need to say *llah ibarç* 'May God bless him', an expression meant to protect against the evil eye.

The first seven days of the child's life are considered the most dangerous. To protect their baby from both the evil eye and the Jinn, Ayt Merghad women perform many protective rites. They consider leaving a newborn alone very risky. They assume that the Jinn can easily exchange their child for the human one, especially if the latter is healthy. If a baby dies within the first seven days of its birth, Ayt Merghad used to automatically attribute the death to the fact that the Jinn had successfully exchanged their baby for theirs.

Other protective actions are taken by women. One of these is to place a knife under their baby's pillow. Ayt Merghad assume that the Jinn dislike white and shiny objects. Therefore, they are kept away by the effect of the knife. Together with the knife, amulets which involve verses from the Quran are commonly used. Women among Ayt Merghad also used to tie a thread of beads and small bag full of salt and *lħrmәl* 'harmal' around the baby's left hand. An old woman justifies this practice by the fact that:

> *"ajt rәbbi ur da ttәṭṭan tisnt, urad qәrbәn adγar nna g tlla. qbәl attәzrit taslmja i waḍḍuns, iħla ad γurs tadʒt isgʷar (tisnt d lħarmәl) qad ttit ħәfḍn ."*

> *"The Jinn do not eat salt; they do not approach the place where you put it. Therefore, before you leave the newborn on its own, it is good to leave 'isgʷar' (salt and harmәl) with it, it will protect it."*

Photo 6. An Ayt Merghad baby's left hand with a bracelet made of black beads, a Hamsa[1] hand and a shell as a protection against the evil eye (2009)

---

[1] A Hamsa is an amulet shaped like a hand, it is thought to protect against the evil eye. In Islam, it is known as the hand of Fatima zahraa, the Prophet's daughter.

Photo 7. A necklace used as a protection against the evil eye (2012)

Ayt Merghad's fear of the evil eye pushes them to put some dirt on the newborn's forehead. When guests come to congratulate the new mother, some of them might be jealous especially if the newborn is a boy, and this feeling is capable of harming the baby. Therefore, to protect the latter from the evil eye, the guests' attention should not be directed to the baby but to something else. As a result, women put some dirt on the baby's forehead as an efficient way to distract the guests' attention. This practice is clearly shown in the following quote made by a 78-year-old woman:

> *"da ttəggan lfasux g twənza i ssabi, da jtrara tiṭ. da tyiman gin awd imiħ n uҁffus g ujrri ns afad tamṭṭut nna di ddan adur tsksiw s ssabi, ad tsksiw s lusx. "*

> *"They put gum ammoniac in the newborn's fringe; it protects it from the evil eye. Sometimes, people even put some ash on its forehead. Any woman who comes will not keep looking at the baby because the dirt will attract her attention."*

Another protective practice among Ayt Merghad is the use of henna. The latter is believed to contain *baraka* 'divine blessing' which has the ability to protect both the mother and the newborn. After giving birth, women use henna to adorn their hands and feet as a protection against any evil. The henna tradition is also applied to the baby. Right after birth the child's body is rubbed with dry henna, which is assumed to provide the baby with its *baraka* and protect it against any evil.

Photo 8. An Ayt Merghad baby's legs adorned with henna with the left one surrounded by an amulet (2009)

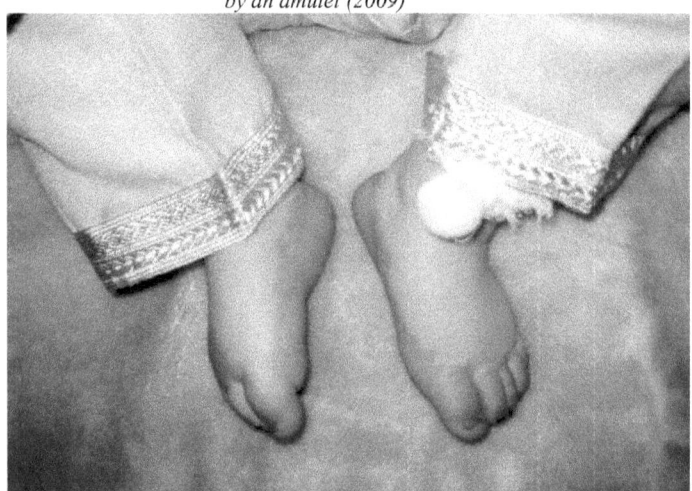

The Celebration: Rites of Incorporation

The sex of the newborn used to determine the time to start the celebration, and the extent of joy to be expressed. If a woman gives birth to a boy, women from the family make seven *tiyʷratin* 'ululations' at the sunrise of the first day. This state is illustrated in the quote below made by a 71-year-old woman:

> *"dilliy mǝk turw tmǝṭṭut l3il, da ttalij ça n tmǝṭṭut s tduli, tǝskǝr sǝb3a n tǝyʷratin. mçid tarbat ajd ilulan ur da ttisllid i tǝyʷratin. ur swa lqima n l3il d tǝrbat. dilliy da ttinin tarbat ur t3ǝmmir adyar. l3il i3mmǝr adyar n bbans. addaj turut tarbat, da txitir tawl ṭffǝy tadʒ lwaldin nǝs."*

> *"In the past, if a woman gave birth to a male baby, a female relative would climb the roof and ululate seven*

44

times. In case, the new born was a female, no ululations were heard. A male's value was never similar to that of a female. People used to claim that a girl would not stay at her parents' home forever. A boy would always assume his father's roles. As for a girl, she would get married once grown up and leave her parents.

Any woman who comes to congratulate is supposed to ululate too. A very good care is taken of *tamzurt* 'a woman who has just given birth'. The family members prepare for her different types of food and insist on her to eat well. On the third day, the family organizes a ceremony during which all the family members are invited and sheep is slaughtered and prepared to be served. *tamzurt* is offered some of what is provided to the guests.

After the mother and the baby's passage through the critical initial transition stage, a new phase begin. On the seventh day after the birth of a boy, the family organizes another ceremony referred to as *ssib3*, during which a number of rites are performed. Sheep is sacrificed on behalf of the baby who subsequently gets a name. In case the grandparents are still alive, they are given the honor to choose the name for the newborn who is, most of the time, named after his grandfather or one of his uncles. After slaughtering the sheep, *ləfqih* 'the imam of the mosque' prepares *asγwi* to protect the baby from the evil eye. *asγwi* is composed of an amulet made from a piece of leather in which verses from the Quran are written, a cowry shell, *luban* 'amber', *matərmumu* 'a multicoloured bead', an almond, a silver coin, a piece of the slaughtered sheep's tail, salt and harmal. The baby is supposed to wear *asγwi* until the age of two.

Photo 9. Sheep is slaughtered on the seventh day (2008)

The family and friends are again invited. The guests are supposed to bring gifts which are mainly in the form of sugar, eggs, or wheat. The family members organize *ahidus* 'a traditional dance accompanied by songs performed by both men and women'; everybody sings and dances. The relatives also do their best to make the ceremony enjoyable. The following *izlan* 'songs' are played:

1. abab n mumu isa3dak rəbbi	1. Oh baby's parents!
2. adig anbark jidir amin	Congratulations!
	2. May your baby be blessed and
3. abu ssibɜ ax iɣran adak asgm	remain alive, Ameen.
mulana	3. Oh our host! May God protect and
	bless your baby.
4. akig rəbbi d lqandil a l3ilinu	4. May God make you my lamp
addik ssadx ibardan ur xuliɖy	which will enlighten unfamiliar
	roads for me.

The song begins by congratulating *tamzurt*. The following lines wish that the baby stays alive and becomes educated and rich in order to help his mother visit places she does not know. The reference here, according to one of the respondents, is made to Mekka. Women sing another song that demonstrates how lucky *tamzurt* is:

46

1. *abab n mummu is3dak rǝbbi tudit naɣ ayu s wudi ttamamt*

2. *a baba ula mma a baba ula mma aḍwad ar ɣuri hat labas ɣuri assa3dinu ufixtin g ulmu almu n iɣbula n waman*

3. *a baba ula mma a baba ula mma ʒʒaʒix zaṛṛun n ʒʒaʒi s rǝbbi*

1. Oh baby's parents! Congratulations! Butter or milk with salted butter and honey.

2. Oh father and mother! Oh father and mother! Come back to me, I am very well, I have found my luck in green fields with water springs.

3. Oh father and mother! Oh father and mother! I rely on you, we rely on God.

To celebrate her passage and that of her son from the initial risky period, *tamzurt* is supposed to put *la3najt* 'make-up'. She adorns her face with *tayamut* 'safron', and outlines her eyes with *tazult* 'kohl'. She then puts *ixǝrban* 'accessories used in the sides of the head to make a specific hair style'.

Source : http://tribusdumaroc.free.fr/aityafelmane.php

tamzurt covers her head with *tasbnijt* (1) 'a red piece of cloth with yellow lines'. Around the head, she ties *taʃddat n muzun* 'a scarf embroidered with beads' and puts *tisddit* (2). On the sides of her head, she puts *ṭwabi3* (4). She also puts *lluban* (5) 'amber', *izbgan* 'bracelets' and *lxəlxal* 'a bracelet put around the ankle'. Finally, she puts *aħzzəmn muzun* 'a belt embroidered with beads'. Some of these are presented in the following photo.

Photo 11. Some of the accessories used by an Ayt Merghad tamzurt

After getting dressed and putting the make-up, *tamzurt* welcomes the guests. Meanwhile, women responsible for cooking prepare for her a special dish made of the sheep's right shoulder. Once the meal is ready, a highly valued man of the family is supposed to serve *tamzurt*. The assumption underlying such a rite is the fact that a woman who managed to give birth to a boy deserves the privilege of being served by a highly respected man in the community. A 67-year-old woman admits that:

> *"addag turw tməṭṭut l3il, da digs thallun ʃijan. ass n ssib3, das ssənwan ajt taddart taɣrut tajffast n unuguḍ. ça n urgaz nna ɣur tlla lqima g tqbilt ajd innan adast jawi."*

> *"When a woman gives birth to a boy, she receives a special treatment. For example, on the seventh day, the family cooks the sheep's right shoulder. The latter is usually served by a man who is highly valued in the community."*

tamzurt further celebrates her transition from the pregnancy state to the one of a mother of a boy by visiting a river. On the celebration day, the father or another member of the family holds the baby and puts it on his mother's back as shown in Photo 13. The former is chosen on the basis of a number of criteria, namely kindness, intelligence, obedience, among other things. The assumption behind such a practice is that these qualities will be transferred to the baby. In this regard, a 62-year-old woman declares that:

> *"argaz nna jnna d igr ssabi s tadawt n mmans as n ssab3, ixssa atili yurs lqima ,ishu, ihlu g rraj ns, afad asska awd nətta addigs jay."*

> *"The man who would place the baby at her mother's back on the seventh day should have a great value. He should be healthy and well-behaved. It was believed that the baby would resemble that man when he grows up."*

---

[2] The baby used to be wrapped in a piece of cloth and swaddled from shoulders to feet.

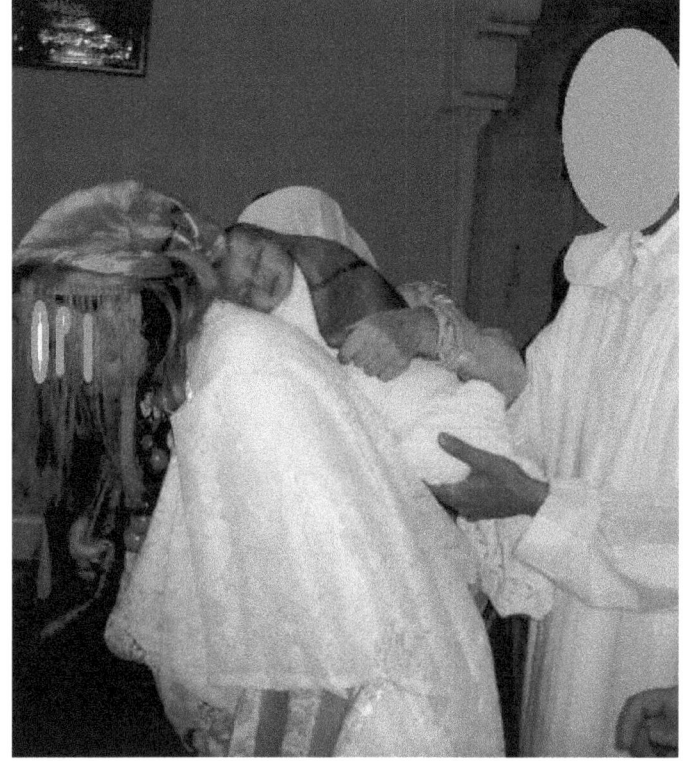

Meanwhile, seven *tiyʷratin* 'ululations' are made. The mother, then, takes *ta3murt* 'a wooden jug' and goes to the river. With the baby on her back, she fills it with water and comes back home. This rite is meant to mark the beginning of a new phase. After the first seven days, the mother is supposed to resume her usual chores. Thus, the visit to the river is the first task to be accomplished. Taking the baby in her back is also highly symbolic. Through this rite, Ayt Merghad view boys as a source of economic utility. Through the act of bringing water, the source of life, the mother implies that her son will become a source of greater security and financial help for his parents in their old age. This assumption is clearly articulated by a 72-year-old woman who claims that:

*"as n ssib3, da təddu təmzurt s asif, tbab l3il nəs,
t3əmmərd ta3murt s waman. hat annajət məddən, hat
turw l3il. hat γurs lqima γur l3il. asska awd ntta qad jazl
xf bbans d mmans, ardi ttawi ṛṛəzq."*

*"On the seventh day, the new mother would go to the
river carrying her baby bat her back. She would fill a
wooden jug with water. People would see her and get the
message that she gave birth to a male baby. The latter
had a great value. When he grows up, he would take care
of his parents and bring them sustenance."*

The last rite is performed forty days after birth. The family organizes the
third ceremony. For a period of forty days after birth, a woman is considered
unclean. At the end of this period, the new mother accomplishes a purification
rite by taking a shower and doing ablutions. When they get up, women of the
family make seven *tiγʷratin* 'ululations', and the relatives are again invited. The
mother will for a second time put *la3najt* 'make up'. The guests are served
couscous and meat. In the afternoon, tea is prepared and served along with
peanuts. Meanwhile, the guests try to create a joyful atmosphere through singing
and dancing.

Conversely, the birth of a girl is not highly welcomed by Ayt Merghad.
Many of the rituals performed after the birth of a boy are eliminated when a girl
is born. The first six days after delivery are characterized by the absence of any
sign of celebration. The relatives make short visits to congratulate the new
mother, but no *tiγʷratin* 'ululations' are made. Members of the family do not
take a good care of *tamzurt*; on the opposite, they direct looks of blame to her.

On the seventh day, a moderate *ssib3* 'a naming ceremony' is organized.
The father of the newborn slaughters sheep and gives a name to his daughter.
The relatives are invited and served couscous and meat. *tamzurt* eats from what
the others are served, and no special food is prepared for her. This state is
clearly articulated in the quotation below:

"ur da feṛṛħən mədn s zzijada n ṭərbat am l3il. ul llint
tɣratin afad sbəjjən afraħ. awd tamzurt ur da diçs thallan
ula jas ʒʒuʒdən çan lmakla ẓaṛs istin. awad ass n ssib3
ur da ittəgga am win l3il."

"Unlike a boy, the birth of a girl is not that appreciated.
There are no ululations to show happiness. The new
mother does not receive much care as no special food is
prepared for her. Also the naming ceremony is not like
that of boy."

Concerning cutting the baby's hair, the father performs this rite only when the infant is one-year-old. The equivalent of the weight of the hair in silver is given as charity. Two hairstyles are common among Ayt Merghad kids between the age of one and two years. For Irbiben, a segment of Ayt Merghad, boys' hairstyle is referred to as *tayəfrijt* 'shaving the head but leaving a single lock of hair on the crown'. Girl's hairstyle includes *taʃṭṭuħt* 'a single lock of hair' at the back of the head and *tawənza* 'a fringe'. For Ayt Hru, another segment among Ayt Merghad, *azag*, a vertical line of hair that runs from the front of the head to the nape of the neck, is a common hairstyle for boys. As for girls, they keep four *tiʃəṭhin* (sg. *taʃəṭṭuħt*) 'locks of hair' on the four sides of the head.

PART THREE: DISCUSSION

Birth and The Evil Eye in The Ayt Merghad Culture

Belief in the destructive effect of the evil eye constitutes an important part of the Ayt Merghad culture. There used to be a strong conviction among the Ayt Merghad community that this supernatural power was behind the high mortality rates among mothers and babies during and after delivery. Moreover, diseases used to be attributed to the evil eye or supernatural powers.

Women giving birth were assisted by a mid-wife who used to have no formal training in health practices but who used to acquire her skills through practice. When she faces a complicated case, she tries to adapt her knowledge. In cases of failure, blame was never put on her; on the contrary, superstition would always be the culprit. A 58-year-old woman who has painful memories about her first and last pregnancy accepted to share her story.

> *"kixtən lliɣ s udis txiṭrij t3əbbut.çul majdi izran ar it3əʒʒab itixitərt nəs. arij ttinin ajt taddart ad lsəɣ i3ban iws3an afd si ffərɣ. dima arij ttinin han tadist nnaɣ ixatərn da dʒəddəd tiṭ. ajnna tbda digi tziri, tɣrajas təmɣart inw i 3ṭṭis nu rgaz inw, nna jwalfə da t3awan tiwtmin nna jran ad jarw. taga ugar n lʒəhd nəs afad uruɣ. tqqima ari t3ssar ta3bbut walajnni ur tqḍi jaḍu. jussa ɣifi uzbar, imih ardi ţfɣən idamn. tnnajasn i ajt taddart hati ixssa ad dduɣ s sbitar fisa3. afan ninawḍ sbitar n mulaɣ 3li frif txəssa jaɣ tassa3t n ubrid. ajnna ni nuwḍ ur iqqimi majd nt3taq. innaj uḍbib içniwn nna jllan g tdist inw mmutn. innajji hat ur imkin ad aruɣ bla lbarasjun. ur ijlly winnaɣ g iɣf 3la ḥqqaf ur dʒin dkkiɣ ɣur uḍbib ajnna da ttaruɣ. ajdəɣ iʒran isbbəb i lmut n içniwn ig awd ssabab ad ur jad ttaruɣ. luqt nnaɣ awd jan ur ilamma tmṭṭuṭ nna j3awən g tarwa walakin ruran majdi iʒran i tiṭ."*

> *"Thirty nine years ago, I was pregnant and my belly was too large, everybody was commenting on its size. The family members insisted on me to wear large clothes to hide it. They kept telling me that my belly was attractive and it might be targeted by the evil eye. With the first signs of delivery, my mother-in-law called my husband's*

aunt, who used to assist women while giving birth. She did her best to help me. She kept pressing on my belly but in vain. The pain was unbearable, suddenly, I started bleeding; only then, did she inform the family members that I urgently needed to be taken to the hospital. It took us an hour to arrive to Moulay Ali Cherif Hospital; unfortunately, we were too late. The doctor told me that I was pregnant with twins but they are dead. He also said that it was not possible for me to give birth without a cesarean section. Of course, I did not know because I did not do any check up during my pregnancy. As a result of that incident, I lost the twins and all the hope of giving birth again. At that time, no one put the blame on the midwife; on the opposite everybody was hinting at the effect of the evil eye."

The belief in the evil eye and the Jinn still exists among Ayt Merghad. They are perceived as fatal forces that can destroy one's life. Therefore, protection from their negative outcomes appears in many forms. In the past, Ayt Merghad used to resort to superstition to counteract these supernatural powers. An old woman states in a very careful tone:

"annag tzajd tsəlmja, daṭrara mmans lbal məzjan. llan məddən nna mi xxant waln. qbal ad ddun ingbawn das ttassa g ufus ajffas lxiṭ nna gllan waqqajn d tkmmist n tisnt d lharmal"

"When a baby was born, the mother should be very very cautious. Some people's looks are harmful. Before the guests arrive, she should tie around the baby's right hand a thread with beads and a small bag full of salt and harmal."

Another 64-year-old woman admits that Ayt Merghad believe that:

"ajt rabbi ur da təṭṭan tisnt, urad qarbən adɣar nna g tlla. qbal attatdʒt taslmja i waḍḍuns, iħla ad ɣurs tsərst isgʷar (tisnt d lharmal) qad tti həfḍn ."

"The Jinn do not eat salt; they do not approach the place where you put it. Therefore, before you leave the baby on

57

its own, it is good to place 'isg^war' (salt and harmal) next
to it as it will protect it."

Recently, education has affected the way the evil eye is being dealt with.

Educated women consider religion an effective means to control the evil eye.

Ayt Merghad assume that the protection from the evil eye can be achieved

through seeking refuge in the Quran. A 25-year-old woman notes that: *"tlla tiṭ,*

ttudkar g lqran, juhn attamz g təslmjiwin. ajnnaɣ as ixssa ad ɣifsn tqqar mma

nsn çu sbaḥ surat lfalaq d nnas." *"The evil eye exists, it is mentioned in the*

Quran, and babies can be easily harmed. Therefore, the mother should read

alfalak and annass chapters for her baby every morning." A 30-year-old woman

also believes that people should seek protection in God; she states that:

> *"hat iḥla ad ttuɣr ruqja xf tslmja. asagd tnçər mmans,*
> *lḥaʒt tamzwarut na ttəgga hija aṭṭasəj taslmja ns tini:*

بسم الله أرقيك ، من كل شيء يؤذيك ، من شر كل نفس أو عين حاسد الله
يشفيك، بسم الله أرقيك . ''

> *"It is very important to read 'ruqja' over a baby. When the*
> *mother gets up the first thing to do is to hold her baby and*
> *say:*
> *In the name of Allah I recite this ruqja over you. From*
> *anything which may harm you, from the evil of every soul*
> *and envious eye, Allah heals you. In the name of Allah I*
> *recite this ruqja on you."*

However, using these methods to counteract the effect of the evil eye does not

exclude the use of other superstitious methods. A 26-year-old woman argues

that:

> *"addag tzajd tsəlmja ixssa aṭḥawlt ad ur digs tamz tiṭ.*
> *iḥla ad ɣifs tɣərt surat lfalaq d surat nnas d iḥla ad as*
> *təgt lḥərz. hati jəḥla, da digs ttilint ɣir ça ləajat n*
> *lqurʔan."*

> *"When a baby was born you should do your best to*
> *protect him from the evil eye. It is good to read alfalaq*
> *and annass chapters, but you can also use an amulet. It is*

good; it just includes a paper in which Quranic verses are written. If an amulet doesn't benefit the baby, it won't harm it."

She also adds that putting the Quran next to the baby is likely to protect it from the evil eye. A similar view is expressed by a 28-year-old woman describing Ayt Merghad's attitudes towards the evil eye. She claims: *"saraħatan, mədn g dadɣ suln da ssəxdamn id lħʒab d tisnt d lħarəml afad ad ur tamz tiṭ g tsəlmjiwin nsən. walakin da ṭṭugant ujdɣ n lumur s tufra. drusn mədn iṭṭinin hat da tənt ttəggan."* *"Frankly, people here are still using amulets, salt and harmel to protect their babies from the evil eye. However, these practices are used in total secrecy, and very few people admit their use."* It can be inferred from the statements above that fear from the evil eye is deeply rooted in the Ayt Merghad's psyche and cannot be easily overcome. The photo below shows the Quran next to a baby with the aim to protect him from the evil eye.

Photo 14. An Ayt Meghad baby with the Quran next to its head (2009)

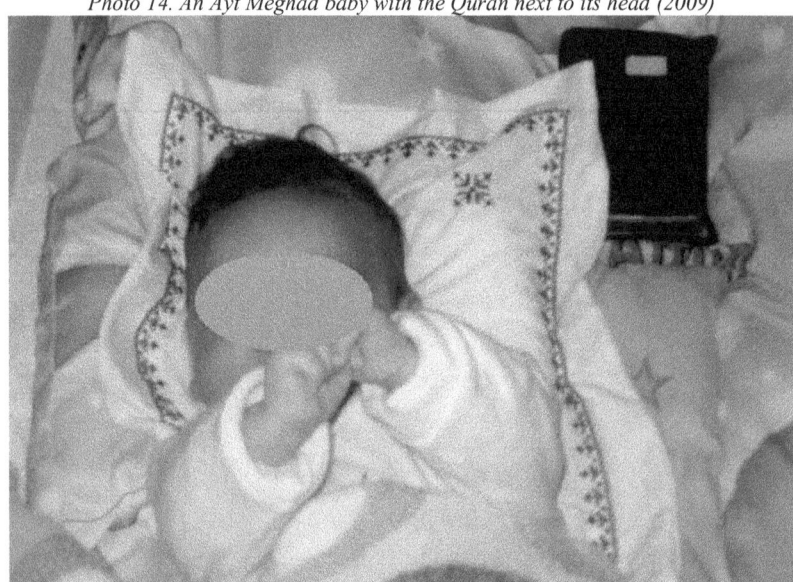

The evil eye beliefs and treatments among Ayt Merghad have not disappeared with urbanization and the access to modern medicine. The respondents claim that the evil eye affects babies and causes a sudden illness. This is a common sign after someone has visited the house. In such a case, the baby is taken to *lfqih* 'a righteous old man' or to *mmi ifilu* 'a woman known for her capacity to remove the effect of the evil eye to neutralize its effect. In this regard, a 74-year-old woman confesses that:

"awd nkkin s iɣfinw, uruɣ taddun juwt tməṭṭut, tnnaji ambark maj tturut. imç daj tffəɣ, jaɣax ça l3il. iga amid islliw, ur iʒrrid ad iṭṭəd. tddud mmi ifilu. tgras ifilu, tinaɣ hat tin idamn nnun, hat dɣi dɣi ayd ikka wannawn digs inharn. tgas ifillu afad as tks tiṭ. da ttasi ifilu tɣar ɣifs qol howa llah çrat tikkal, tssutl tid i jiɣf n tssəlmja, tasitid tssutlt i tifdnt nəs təɣras qol howa llah çrat tikkal. luqt nna jks hat təks tiṭ."

"I, myself, gave birth, and a woman came to congratulate me. As soon as she left, the baby felt sick, he

was pale and unable to suck my breast. 'mmi ifilu' (a woman known for her capacity to remove the effect of the evil eye) came. After she examined the baby using a thread, she told us that the baby was evil eyed by one of our female relative who had just left. In order to exorcise the baby, 'mmi ifilu' took the thread, and she recited al ixlas chapter three times. Then, she encircled the thread around the baby's head. She, then, tied it to her toe and recited the same chapter three times. Once the thread got unfastened from the toe, it means that the effect of the evil eye has been removed."

Another old woman states that:

"addag jaɣ ça tasəlmja, dat nṭṭawij s ɣur lfqih. afad as iks tiṭ, dajggar imiħ n ʃʃəb gʷ afa, daj bəddər ism n rabbi d lanbija d lawlija. addag iɣra ça n lʔajat n lquran, das jakka imma n tsəlmja lħarz aṭṭi təg g waman tssərd zarsən tasəlmja"

"When a baby is sick as a result of the evil eye, we take it to lafqih 'a righteous old man'. To exorcise the evil eye from the body of the baby, he puts pieces of alum into fire, and then he pronounces the name of God, his Prophets and righteous ones, and recites verses from the Quran. He gives the mother an amulet and asks her to put it in some water and use the latter to wash the baby."

According to a 33-year-old-woman, a similar practice is still being used. She states that: "mç tʃkka tməṭṭut is tumz tiṭ g tsəlmja nəs, da tqqar rruqja xf imiħ n waman tssird as zarsən.""If a woman suspects that her baby has been affected by the evil eye, she reads 'ruqja' over some water and uses the latter to wash her baby". She justifies such practices by saying that 'ruqja' was used by the prophet (peace be upon him).

Another practice is still used by Ayt Merghad to treat the effect of the evil eye. People still believe that lbxur 'incence' is efficient in healing the person affected by the evil eye. To exorcise the evil eye from the body of the patient, lbxur made of ʃʃəbb 'alum' is used because its transformation has a strong magical impact. It is assumed that as the alum is transformed by fire, the effect of the evil eye is neutralized.

Ayt Merghad strongly believe that the evil eye is a destructive power that can extremely harm or cause death to people. They also assume that pregnant women and babies are the most vulnerable to it. Indeed, the belief in the evil eye is not exclusive to the Ayt Merghad culture; different cultures of the world hold similar convictions. For example, in the Middle East:

> *"the main general characteristics of the evil eye are that it relates to the fear of envy on the eyes of the beholder, and that its influence is avoided or counteracted by means of devices calculated to distract its attention and by practices of sympathetic magic."* (Spooner 1976: 77)

As Spooner (1976) states, the most vulnerable people to the evil eye are children, brides and pregnant women. The evil eye is believed to cause sickness, fatigue and even death. The people targeted are mainly children and those who are extremely beautiful or healthy (Shiloh, 1961).

The belief in the evil eye, as a destructive power, is a significant aspect of the Ayt Merghad culture. With respect to pregnancy and birth, it has constituted a major factor in accounting for any malevolence. However, women's education has largely influenced the way the evil eye is perceived and dealt with in the community.

Gender Preferences among Ayt Merghad

The preference of boys over girls has been a strong aspect of the Ayt Merghad culture. A 55-year-old woman states that:

> *"ɣur ajt mərɣad, təlla lqima bəzzaf ɣur iʃirran. ajnnaɣ axf da ttəggan itsənt l3wajd am lfal i təslit afad ad ttarw iʃirran. luqt nna ɣʷman i təslit, da ttasin lħanna nna di ʃajḍən gənt aflla n iɣf i iʃirran afad atni ttarw."*

> *"In the Ayt Merghad community, boys are highly valued. That is why they practice certain rites as an omen for the*

bride to have boys. For example, after the bride puts henna, they take the henna left and put it on the head of boys so that she will give birth to males."

The strength of this preference is justified by financial, social and psychological factors. Economically speaking, men hold more economic power; therefore, parents gain more financial benefit from sons than from daughters. Male children are more capable of providing assistance in agriculture, the main activity in the past; whereas, girls can only help with household tasks or care for younger siblings; a state which was not financially rewarding. While daughters are seen as a source of monetary cost, boys grew up to become a source of an economic benefit for their parents. This assumption is clearly stated by a 75-year-old Ayt Merghad woman who says: *"ajnna tṣərft f tʃarratin hat xlifa 3la llah. da txitirnt awəlnt fɣənt taddart n lwaldin nsənt. walajnni iʃirran daç ttasin g təwsər."* *"Whatever you pay for girls is never rewarded; they just grow up to get married and leave their parents' house; whereas, boys support you in your old age".* Another 58-year-old woman states that:

> *"dilliɣ tarbaṭ hat awṭhaḥ, tga am tsəmxt. ur da txaddəm, ur tgi tin ʃwar. ɣir atxdəm nnit, tqabəl taddart. ar təgga ajnna s inna urgaz dɣi gas tlla tnbaṭ g ufus. tamṭṭut ur ɣurs tla ssulta. awd am3rad mək dast jakka at fəst. lmuhim tamṭṭut hat awṭhaḥ, hat am tsəmxt. g lmital, məç tʃan irgzən ṭṭaʒin nəɣ swan ataj, ur nnin ad inin hat tamṭṭut tqqiman afad adas adʒən amur nəs. tturbba ṭərbat s g təmzi ad ttgga ajnnas inna urgaz swa iga g bbans nəɣd ajt mas. addag tuwl hat imçinna ajd illan gras d urgaz nəs. dɣi g twalf ajnnaɣ n lhalt, urdʒin asd iddi ffiʃkəl."*

> *"In the past, a girl was valueless, and she was like a slave. She would not get a job, and nobody would consult her. She had to do all the domestic chores and obey her husband since he was the only decision maker. A woman had no authority. If her husband beat her, she had to accept that. A woman had no value, and she was just like a slave. For example, if men ate ṭṭaʒin or drank tea, they*

would not bother leaving some to the women. A girl is
educated to obey men in her family be them her father or
brothers. When she gets married, it is the same story with
her husband. Since she is used to that mode of life, she
never finds the situation abnormal."

A 69-year-old woman shares a similar view:

"juf l3il ṭarbat. l3il qad ɣifm jazl. addag txaṭər ṭərbat qa
ttawl tddu s ça n txamt jaḍn. l3il hat winm ajd iga abda.
ajnna tsarft f ṭarbat hat idda."

"A boy is better than a girl, the former will support you.
When a girl grows up, she gets married and joins another
family. A boy is always yours. What ever you pay for a
girl will never be rewarded."

Therefore, in such a community where agriculture is the main activity, the
economic obligations of male children towards their parents are great. Sons,
unlike daughters, are considered the family pillars because they ensure
protection of the family land. They, therefore, are considered the family source
of income as they have to support their parents in their old age.

As a patriarchal community, Ayt Merghad also value sons for social
reasons. Families' strong desire to have boys emanates from the fact that the
latter carry on the family name. At the psychological level, giving birth to a boy
offers the parents some kind of internal stability. Having sons makes both the
father and the mother feel proud of themselves. A family without a son is looked
down on by the community, and is dealt with as an incomplete entity. In fact,
both parents suffer in such a situation, but it is the mother who bears the whole
responsibility. The gender of the newborn decides the status and position of the
mother in the household. A woman who does not have a son is ill-treated by her
husband and his family. Therefore, women keep on having children until they
have a boy. This state is made explicit by a 53-year-old woman in the quotation
below:

"mmi jʃirran da ttəħlu ɣur imɣarn, da ttəħlu ɣur urgaz. ur da ttəgga mmi jʃirran d m tʃarratin kif kif. tlla juwt tməṭṭut imarḍən s imʃinnay nnit, da tsksij hat llant g jiwt taddart han tady ar ttarw iʃirran han nttat da ttarw tiʃarratin, han tadday çanas lqima tħlu ɣurs kulʃi, han nttat ttuħgar."

"The woman who gives birth to boys is admired by her parents-in-law and her husband. The mother of boys is never similar to that of girls. There was a woman who got sick because of this preference. She had only daughters and used to live with her brother-in-law's wife who had boys. The latter was highly valued and favoured by everybody unlike the former who was always despised."

Another 61-year-old woman claims that:

"ur ɣursənt dwa dilliy, baʃ ad ħddant. da ttarunt ard ifukkw usddi. məç t3aṭṭər baʃ attarw l3il , qa təg ça n ssibab baʃ atti tarw. g ssat da tzurənt sidi 3bdllah. illa jiwn, ssənxt, turw as tamṭṭut rab3a n tʃarratin, ininas lwaldin nəs ixssa atiwlt baʃ attarut l3il. jawl, iddu s ḍḍariħ n sidi 3abdllah. ddun zurn n3mnas, mç jurw l3il dasd ittawi tiɣərsi. ajnna urw, urw tarbat."

"Women had no idea about contraceptives. A woman would be giving birth until they reach the menopause. If she was late in giving birth to a male, she had to do something. In my village, women would visit the mausoleum of Sidi Abdellah. I know a man whose wife gave birth to four girls. His parents asked him to marry another woman so as to have a boy. He got married a second time and went to visit the mausoleum of Sidi Abdellah. He promised the dead 'wali' to bring an animal to sacrifice if he had a boy. When his second wife gave birth, she also had a daughter."

A similar view is expressed by a 57-year-old woman:

mmi jiʃirran təlla ɣurs lqima, maʃi am tanna jttarun tiʃirratin. dilliy, llan medən mçtən isaqsa ça 'maj tturw

*flanta?' daj ṭṭini 'turw ajnna ṭnnum', iʒawbas 'turwt diɣ
allah rabbi'. awd ad inin 'tarbat' ur dat ttinin.*

*"The woman who gives birth to boys has more value than
the one who gives birth to girls. In the past, when some
people were asked about a woman who has just given
birth to a girl' they would answer 'she gave birth to what
she is accustomed to. The one who asked would comment
'oh my God! She gave birth to her again.' They would
not even bother to call the newborn 'a girl'."*

However, due to the urbanization of the Ayt Merghad area, the economic
reason for boy preference no longer seems feasible. Female schooling and the
diversification of the economic activities have to a great extent affected the
traditional negative attitudes towards giving birth to a girl. Access to education
by itself is not enough to eliminate values associated with gender preference
held by the community under study; however, it has largely contributed to the
improvement of the females' status. Education has enabled women to gain
access to male-dominated areas of work and participate in the household
expenses. Education has offered Ayt Merghad females the opportunity to be
less dependent on and more equal to males financially speaking. This
assumption is clearly articulated by a 36-year-old woman who states that:

*"ur illi lfərq gər iʃirran d tʃərratin. dɣi da qqarənt
tʃərratin, ɣijnt ad waḍḍəfənt. ur jad ħtaʒʒant ad qqimənt
g taddart ar tgannant ad awəlnt. wahli n tʃərratin da
xddəmnt ar t3awanənt bba nsənt d l3aʔilat nsənt."*

*"There is no difference between sons and daughters.
Girls go to school today and can even obtain work
outside the home. They are no longer supposed to stay at
home and wait for a husband. Many girls are working
and helping their fathers with the family expenses."*

Another 28-year-old woman assumes that:

*"ur jad illi lfərq gər iʃirri d tarbat. ikkatən l3il nttan ajd
ittasint taddart çullu. dɣi da tqqar ṭərbat tssən kulʃi; tiɣi*

attəxdəm awd nttat. maħd tarbat awd nttat da txaddəm
hat ur jad iqqimi lfərq."

"There is no longer a difference between a boy and a
girl. A son was the one who assumed the family's
responsibility. Nowadays, a girl has access to schooling,
she knows everything, and therefore, can work. Since a
girl can get a job, the difference between a male and a
female no longer exists."

Currently, Ayt Merghad express their wish to have both sons and boys
and girls. Nevertheless, sons are considered essential while daughters are not.
Most parents-to-be of a first child state that the child's gender does not matter,
but most of those who do express a preference would prefer a son. The wish to
have a second child with a specific gender is determined by the first child's
gender. When a couple already has one child, the desire to have a second one
with the opposite gender is highly expressed. This desire seems stronger among
the parents who already have a daughter than those who already have a son.
Nevertheless, the reasons behind son preference have lost credibility. The
diversification of the economic activities, the increased rates of girls' schooling
and women's access to the job market have shaken the negative attitudes Ayt
Merghad used to have towards giving birth to girls.

The Loss of Birth Rites and Urbanization

Recently, the Ayt Merghad area has witnessed a number of mutations. The latter have led to the disappearance of most of the birth-related practices among the members of the community. Education has played a vital role in this process. Statistically speaking, female schooling in Ferkla has significantly improved during the last decades. According to the results of the 1960 census, 99% of the rural population in Morocco was illiterate. In 2004, female schooling rate in Ferkla reached 43.5%. One of the outcomes of educating girls in the target area is that the age of marriage and pregnancy are delayed. Girls who attend primary and secondary school are less likely to get married at an early age. Pregnancy will consequently happen at rather an advanced age.

Before getting pregnant, Ayt Merghad women find themselves more aware of the reproductive health issues. Education has increased their health awareness; and equipped them with knowledge about contraceptives and methods of family planning. Instead of believing in the traditional explanations for the risks surrounding pregnancy and birth, women, now, understand that having births too close together does not allow the mother's body to recover from the strain of previous pregnancies and childbirths. A short interval between pregnancies ends up with the mother taking care of many children at the same time, a matter which exhausts her body and deprives the kids from getting enough care. A 45-year-old woman points out that:

> *"zman tiwtmin da ttarunt wahli n tarwa ula daj ttili gratsən wahli n isggʷasn. ça daj ttəddər ça daj ttəmtat. ur ssinənt aḍu ɣif mawani3 lḥaml nɣəd lfəq gər tidusa. da ttarunt ard wsirənt. dɣi tiwtmin da ssant lkninat nɣəd da ssəxdamənt llawlab. ur da ṭṭarunt wahli n tarwa ar ṭṭili ɣursənt luqt aṭni qabəln."*

> *"Women used to have closely spaced pregnancies and give birth to many kids. Some of them live and some die! They had no idea about contraceptives or birth spacing,*

they just keep giving birth until they become old. Today,
women either take the pill or use a sterilet. They do not
have many children and they have enough time to take
care of them."

With women's awareness of the scientific aspect of pregnancy, the risk of losing the foetus, which was greater in the past, is less of an issue today. Worries are no longer about the evil eye and the Jinn, but concerns are more about the risks of diseases and malformations. Therefore, medical assistance has become highly sought. This shift in the way Ayt Merghad women perceive and interpret the risks of pregnancy is undoubtedly grounded in education, for

"more educated women may be less likely to accept
traditional explanations for life and death and instead
take on broad information about birth spacing, the signs
of pregnancy complications and the need to improve their
nutritional status to reduce the risk of iron deficiency
anemia, all of which are of key importance in the drive to
reduce maternal deaths." (Karlsen, et al., 2011)

Education has also raised Ayt Merghad women's awareness of the benefits of the pre-natal check-ups and infants' immunization. They are more enthusiastic about the health services the public health centers offer. Pregnant women have regular check-ups, and most of them are aware of the benefits of vitamin tablets; therefore, they are more willing to take them. Women in the area are also aware of the usefulness of vaccinating their children. The following quotes illustrate this change in women's mentality. A 32-year-old woman explains that: *"aɣulnt tʷwtmin ɣrant, ɣijnt ad ɣrint tawriqt n uḍbib. addag daṭṭarunt, da tddunt s sbitar ar ttasint lvitaminat mç tnti ħtadʒant.""Women have become educated; they can read a doctor's prescription. During pregnancy, they frequently visit the hospital and take vitamins if needed."*

69

Another 24-year-old woman adds:

> *"urjad tqqimi təmṭṭut nawri ṭggan tsgnit i warrawns. aɣuln w3an mədən s lfajt n tisgnit. idɣ d awd akkan sbitarat tisgna fabur, ur iqqimi l3udr ɣur lawaldin afad ur awin arraw nsən s dinnaɣ."*

> *"I don't think there still exists in the area a woman who does not vaccinate her children. People become more conscious and aware of the benefits of vaccination. Since the hospitals offer vaccines for free, there is no reason why parents should not take their kids there."*

Indeed, as Karlsen et al. (2011) argue:

> *"Increasing levels of educational attainment are likely to enhance the capacity of women to obtain, process and understand basic health information about the benefits of good prenatal care and the reproductive health services needed to make appropriate health decisions."*

The mass media have also played a pivotal role in raising the Ayt Merghad people's awareness about birth-related issues. The latter include birth spacing, contraceptives, prenatal consultations and vaccinations. In the last fifty years, the mass media influence has tremendously grown with the advance of technology. First, there was the radio, then the television and the satellite dish and now the internet. The Ayt Merghad area is characterized by a good access to communication devices. According to the 2004 census, 85.6% of the houses in the target area own a television and 52% have a satellite dish.

During the last decades, there have been major efforts to use the mass media to promote notions of the family planning. Messages in the mass media are aimed at creating general awareness of small family norms. The health ministry, for example, organises various health campaigns with the aim of developing public awareness of the risk of closely-spaced pregnancies and promoting family planning acceptance. Therefore, the radio and TV broadcast programs to persuade women of the personal and social advantages of having smaller families.

A number of studies provide evidence for the fact that the individuals' exposure to mass media messages promoting family planning influences contraceptive behavior (Piotrow et al., 1990; Bankole et al., 1996; Westoff and Bankole, 1997; and Kincaid 2000). Thus, exposure to family planning messages in the media has influenced the Ayt Merghad women's contraceptive behaviour; this is reflected in their desire for fewer children and appreciation of the health and economic benefits of a smaller family. For example, the television broadcasts images which idealize a small family. In this regard, a family with few children is often portrayed as being happier, healthier and more comfortable than a larger family. This is clearly illustrated by the following statement made by a 37-year-old woman:

> *"assa dan taffad təlfaza g çu taddart. da tlmadn məddin bzzaf n lħwaჳ g id lbaramiჳ. matalan, aɣulnt təwtmin ssnənt lʔahammija n wad drassn ifirran. da ditsabajan təlfaza tiwtmin nna ɣur drusn ifirran tsħa tg taЗsrijt. ar di sbajan tanna ɣur ggudin ifirran am çan tmṭṭut ur iɣrin."*

> *"Today a TV set is found in every house. People learn a lot from the programs of different channels, for example, women are now aware of the advantages of having fewer children. The TV broadcasts programs which show that women with fewer children are healthier and more modern. A woman with many children is often presented in films and series as an illiterate woman."*

The mass media messages have, therefore, resulted in a change in the Ayt Merghad people's way of thinking through the diffusion of new ideas and practices related to birth.

Another key factor behind the disappearance of the traditional birth rituals in the Ayt Merghad area is intermarriage. Marriage in the target community used to be governed by rules of endogamy. However, contact between the Ayt Merghad community and people from different ethnicities and cultures has dramatically influenced the prevalent endogamous system of marriage in the area. Therefore, cases of mixed marriage are getting common in the community. Due to rural exodus and immigration abroad, young people from the target community can find a spouse belonging to different ethnic groups.

Until recently, intermarriage was discouraged among Ayt Merghad; whereas, endogamous marriages were highly valued. This trend is being increasingly challenged by the urbanization and modernization process the area has witnessed. In Urban areas, for example, Ayt Merghad live in close proximity to people with different cultural and social norms; however, sharing a similar educational background or other interests has increased the likelihood of dating and marrying. The implication is that tribal boundaries have weakened and cultural barriers have been overcome. Indeed, marriage between members of the target community and those of different cultural backgrounds means that contact with other cultures has resulted in an increased acceptance of the other's culture. The potential implications of intermarriage arguably are much larger. Intermarriage commingles two different cultural backgrounds resulting in the adoption of non-native values and practices.

Many studies depict intermarriage as a key cause behind the loss of the traditional customs and rituals (Crohn, 1995; Kennedy, 2003; Petsonk & Remsen, 1988; Root, 2001). In the analysis if the current state of the birth rituals among Ayt Merghad, the factor of intermarriage has been found to be of central importance. Sometimes, cultural and social norms of the two spouses may be so diametrically opposed. As a result, the likelihood that the couple will adopt new patterns and practices becomes higher. In the case of the target community, the influence of other cultures through intermarriage has resulted in the gradual disappearance of a number of birth rituals. In this regard, a 42-year-old woman argues that:

*"luqt nna g juwl bnadm s bərra n təqbilt, ur jad ittiyi ad
ig yir l3wajd nəs. ixssa dajman adi ggar ajnnatn isman,
walakin ḍaruri da təyllab juwt l3iht. maj ttʒrun howa ku
jan qad isamħ ʃwij, çu jan ig imiħ g l3wajd nəs amma baʃ
ad igər l3wajd nəs mja f lmja hat majmkənʃ."*

*"In cases of mixed marriage, you can no longer practise
your own traditions. The two parties have to practise
what is common between them. What happens is that
each has to make concessions. One cannot keep his/her
traditions 100%."*

Another Ayt Merghad woman, aged 36, confesses that her non-Ayt Merghad
sister-in-law holds a negative attitude towards some of her community's birth-
related practices. She states that:

*"urtgi juwt tmṭṭut n ijma utməryad. txatərd g ṛṛbaḍ ar
tarw dima g lklinik. ur tnni at qbel aṭṭarw g taddart tadr i
timattin. mər tgi ut tmazirt, urtnni attini uho i wijdy n
l3wajd n tmazirt .walajnni ijmanw axattar d tmṭṭut nəs,
nna jgan ut məryad, zdyən g məçnas. wa lajnni twalf ad
tarw g taddart n imyarn nəs. addag as təħḍar tarwa da
təddu s yur imyarn nəs g rrafidija. da ttarw g taddart s
um3awn n mma. ur tnni tslit jaḍn atqbl ajnnay. hat
txatərd g juwn udghar ixtalfn d urdʒin tzri tamṭṭut attarw
g taddart. ajnnagh as ur igi l3ʒəb məç ur tqbil tarwa n
taddart."*

*"One of my sisters-in-law is not from the Ayt Merghad
community as she is from Rabat. She always gives birth
in a private clinic. It is inconceivable for her to give birth
at home or bury the placenta. However, if she were from
my tribe, she would not refuse my community's
traditional practices. For example, my eldest brother and
his wife, who is from the Ayt Merghad community, are
living in Mekness. However, she used to give birth at my
parents' house. It was customary for her to go to her in-
laws house in Errachidia when her due date approaches.
She used to give birth at home under my mother's
supervision. A thing that the other sister-in-law cannot
accept, but I understand her attitude. She has grown up
in a different context. She has never seen a woman giving*

birth at home, so it is not surprising if she considers the
practice as a strange act."

The birth system among Ayt Merghad used to require a number of practices. It was customary for women in the community to give birth at home. This state of affair was associated with a set of ritualistic practices. A case in point is the burial of the placenta. Pregnancy used to be considered a vulnerable period. Because of the high mortality rates among mothers and babies during and after delivery, pregnancy was dealt with a lot of caution. Maternal and infant mortality was attributed to issues related to superstition, the jinn and the evil eye. Not surprisingly, many rituals were performed to protect the mother and the newborn.

However, the improvement in the health services in the southern central areas in Morocco has largely influenced the maternal and infant death rates. This has, in turn, affected the birth rituals among Ayt Merghad. Today, Ayt Merghad pregnant women benefit from free access to prenatal consultations and gynaecological exams. This has certainly encouraged them to make frequent visits to the hospital and receive an appropriate prenatal care. According to the 2004 census, 57.5% of the births in the southern central areas are assisted by a skilled birth attendant. This has undoubtedly contributed to the decrease in maternal and infant mortality rate. With the increased access to hospitals after the independence, the infant mortality rates have witnessed a radical decrease according to the World Bank Report (2011). It decreased from 91 per 1000 born-alive in 1980 to 40 in 2003. The following figure illustrates the significant decrease in infant mortality rates in Morocco for the period between 1976 and 2010.

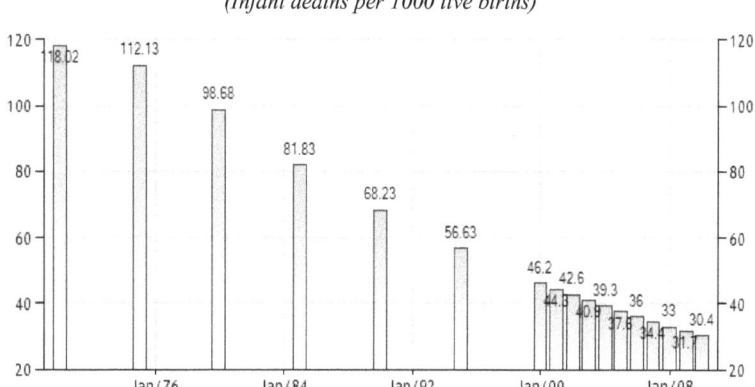

Figure 3. Infant mortality rate in Morocco, 1976-2010
(Infant deaths per 1000 live births)

Source: World Bank Report (2011)

Recently, the Ayt Merghad area has witnessed some development at the level of health services. The province of Errachidia has four public hospitals with a capacity of 593 beds. They are also equipped with advanced materials and skilled stuff. The area also has 29 health centres and 35 rural dispensaries. The following table provides more information about the public sanitary establishments.

Table 5. Public sanitary establishments in Errachidia

	Hospitals		UHCD	UHC	CHCD	CHC	RD
	Number	Beds					
Errachidia	4	593	5	8	16	21	35

Source: Health Ministry (2011)

UHCD : Urban Health Centre with beds for delivery

UHC : Urban Health Centre

CHCD : Communal Health Centre with beds for delivery

CHC : Communal Health Centre

RD : Rural Dispensary

At the level of Ferkla, Ibrahim Al Amrawi Health Centre offers multiple services to pregnant women, among which delivery under a close medical supervision.

Photo 15. Ibrahim Al Amrawi health centre in Tinjdad (2011)

Consequently, most of Ayt Merghad women, especially the educated ones, reject the idea of giving birth at home. A 28-year-old-educated mother states that:

*"llan dγi sbitarat nmalan. γran mədn, aγuln w3an, ssən
is tuf tarwa n sbitar tin taddart. qa ṭṭarw salma, ur inni
ad jili lmuʃkil. ur nniγ nççin, matalan, ad uruγ g taddart,
ʒʒəm3d tiwtmin afad issurunt, 3arraḍaγ iγfinw d umẓẓan
inw i lxaṭar, ntta illa sbitar γir tamanw."*

*"Now the hospitals are close. People are now educated
and aware that it is better to give birth at the hospital
than doing so at home. Women deliver their baby safely
without any problems. For example, I would not give
birth at home with the help of a group of woman
exposing myself along with the baby to risks; whereas a
hospital is nearby."*

In hospitals, the umbilical cords and placenta are discarded as insignificant trash. Accordingly, the mother ends up having no idea about the placenta, and feels no need to ask about it. Subsequently, the ritualistic burial of the placenta together with all the beliefs surrounding this practice have been abandoned.

Giving birth at the hospital entails the loss various practices that used to be associated with birth. This state is discussed in the following quote made by a 32-year-old woman:

*"l3wajd nnak imun d tarwa n taddart ħidənt. am l3at n
tmattin, am ssabi jallah izajd təgtas lħanna ur jad
tqqima, dγi das tdəwwaʃn, am tazult urat jad tggan i
waln n ssabi, assass n jixf ur jad iqqimi, hati jkkatn
ḍaruri. awd tiyʷratin ur jad qqimənt."*

*"The rituals which used to accompany delivery at home
are disappearing. These include the placenta ritual and
putting the henna to the baby. Now the baby is washed.
Also, kohl is no longer put on the baby's eyes. Coiling the
baby's head and ululating have also vanished."*

In hospitals, birth attendants encourage Ayt Merghad women to give up the traditional birthing position and adopt the supine one. The latter requires the birthing mother to be placed on her back with her feet in stirrups, forcing her to push the child out of the birth canal without the aid of gravity. Pain and discomfort are increased and the labor time is extended; as a result, the risk for medical intervention increases drastically. This tendency to substitute the traditional practices in relation to the birthing position can be explained by the fact that birth attendants benefit from training programmes which favour the supine position; hence demonstrating an aspect of the western culture.

Adopting modern ways of doing things at the expense of the traditional alternative is not always a rewarding act. It has been scientifically proven that the supine position is not an ideal position for birth. There is a widespread acceptance of the advantages of adopting an upright position while giving birth (Bhardwaj et al., 1995; Mathews et al., 2005; Roberts & Hanson, 2007; and WHO 1996). It has been shown that such a position shortens the pushing phase of labor by helping the baby drop as far as possible with less effort. Scientifically, it has been proven that squatting is a beneficial birth position as it opens the pelvis while using the gravity to help the baby descend (Saravanan et al., 2010). This position uses the gravity to maximize the effectiveness of the contractions while minimizing the mother's efforts.

Attitudes towards the attendance of males during the birth process have also witnessed a major change. Childbirth used to be viewed as a strictly female affair, and the presence of males a taboo. Nowadays, women among Ayt Merghad no longer radically refuse the presence of a male doctor in the delivery room. However, this tolerance is conditioned. The respondents express no objection towards the presence of a male while giving birth, when there is no alternative. One of the respondents claims that *"məç as tʃəqqa tarwa i təṭṭut tili g lxaṭar, luqt naɣ ur ihmma id argaz mid tamṭṭut ajts iʒʒənʒamn."* *"if a birthing woman is in a risky situation, it doesn't matter if it is a woman or a man who saves her."* Therefore, the risk factor seems to justify the acceptance of a male attendant. The respondents agree on the fact that being supervised by a female is the best situation.

The young generations no longer adhere to the traditional rituals and are seriously questioning them. They do test the validity of certain practices against their new educational background, and when no logical justification is found for some customs, they are abandoned. For example, it used to be a custom to avoid talking about or preparing things for the coming baby. Today, gynecological ultrasound imaging has become a routine part of care for pregnant women among Ayt Merghad. The ultrasound technique is used to observe the baby and check any abnormality. It is also used to determine the baby's gender. Once the latter is determined, Ayt Merghad couples, like all parents, enthusiastically start buying clothes for the coming baby. This action reflects the new generation's deep conviction that the belief that preparing things for the baby beforehand might bring bad lack is a groundless one. Eventually, Ayt Merghad believe that the risks surrounding pregnancy can be avoided through a good medical care.

During the process of modernization, the diversification of the economic activities and the increased access to education have resulted in frequent population mobility in the Ayt Merghad area. Consequently, this has caused more contact with other cultures. Historically, migration in the Ayt Merghad community has involved mainly males, and when women move it is largely as men's companions. In the contemporary era of globalisation, the current migration scene has become characterized by an increasing involvement of the Ayt Merghad women. Frequently, the latter leave their home mainly for two reasons, either to pursue their studies or find a job. This increased migration of women has exposed them to a range of new, non-traditional ideas and to a wider range of people from different ethnic groups. Moreover, the potential for abandoning the old values and rituals increases is in urban areas. Migration has also led women to assume different roles in the home area when they return. This state is reflected in the following quote made by a 40-year-old woman.

"tzzərj illi taxatart rbə3 snijn g mçnas. dɣi datxddəm g fes. ur tgi am isttmas jaḍn. təssən wahli n məddən. tləmd ɣur sən bəzzaf n lumur. mtalan, g tarwanw tamggarut, tənnaj wallu ixssa ad izɛrx aḍbib d ixssa ad sqssay xf luqt n tarwa. idsn wussan qbl ad arruɣ, təddad. ɣir təbda tzirri, tawji s sbittar afad diçs arruɣ. çulfi arrawin qbəl luland g taddart."

"My eldest daughter spent four years at the faculty in Mekness, and now she is working in Fes. She is not like her other sisters. She knows a lot of people and she has learnt a lot from them. For example, during my last pregnancy, she used to insist on me to go to the hospital to do some check-ups. She also insisted on me to ask the doctor about my due date. A few days before the expected time, she came, and with the first sign of labor, she took me to the hospital. It was the first time I give birth at the hospital; all my children were born at home."

Equally important, leaving home often involves moving away from the immediate control and assistance of the traditional patriarchal family. Migration is often associated with migrants becoming independent earners as opposed to workers in agriculture in the family land under the control of the father. The consequent breakdown of the family as the key unit of economic production has certainly loosened the patriarchal authority and the dominance of the extended family. Therefore, migration in the Ayt Merghad area has resulted in the movement from the extended type of family to a nuclear one. Migration has led to the separation of the family members, creating a greater dependence on the nuclear family. This has in turn influenced the traditional birth rituals. For example, giving birth under the supervision of an old member of the family is no longer an automatic act. As a result, assistance is sought at the hospital. In this regard, a 45-year-old woman admits that:

"ajnna juwlaɣ, zzriɣ sin isʷggasn g taddart n imɣarn. uruɣ l3il amzwarru g taddart. təqabl təmɣart kulfi. ur ħtaʒʒay ad dduɣ s ssbitar. Walajnni ajnna ddiɣ s ɣur

urgaz inw s ṛṛəbaḍ, nlla ɣir nʷçni. ajnnaɣ as uruɣ iʃirran jaḍn g ssbitar."

"When I got married, I spent the first two years with my in-laws. I gave birth to my first kid at home. My mother-in-law took care of everything. I didn't need to go to the hospital. However, when I joined my husband in Rabat, we were living alone. Therefore, I had to give birth to the other kids at the hospital."

Another 31-year-old woman claims that:

"laɣlabija n l3wajd ṛtabṭənt s udɣar. matalan afad uruɣ l3il ixssa ad ẓurɣ juwn ḍḍariḥ. mç lliɣ g təmdint, waxxak riɣ atti ẓurɣ, hat ur jad imkini. g tmazirt da tʃbbarn twətmin g tgatut jugəln g tigȝda n ssəqf addag rant ad urunt, g təmdint ur illi wjnnaɣ. matalan timattin artənti nttadər g agənsu n ləɣbar, g təmdint, hat majmkənʃ."

"The majority of rituals are linked to the place of residence. For example, to give birth to a boy, I have to visit a mausoleum. If I live in a city, I cannot do that. In the village, people use a rope hanged to the beams of the roof while giving birth, a thing which does not exist in cities. Also, we bury the placenta in the stable, which is impossible in cities."

Another aspect which has been affected by urbanization and the socio-economic mutations Morocco has recently witnessed is the infant's naming process. Many respondents have stated that only very few parents stick to the use of Amazigh names while most of the members of the Ayt Merghad community are more opting for the use of modern names for their children. Most parents choose common names instead of the Amazigh traditional names. For example, names like 'Moha', 'Hṛou', 'Iṭṭou', 'Hdda' and 'Hannou' are being abandoned in the community. Migration and contact with non-Amazigh people have exposed the target community to different cultures and languages. This has brought about the introduction of new names in the Ayt Merghad community. In this regard, a 28-year-old-educated mother claims that:

"ur gix i tarwanw ismawn n iʃəlħijn baʃ adur ttumijjazn. maħd iʃirri jlla g juwn udɣar urid wins ajd iga, ang ismawn nna jllan g udɣar nna. saraħat ammi ur nəṛḍi s lasl nəɣ. mlad is tʃəbbətx s l3adat n tmazirtinw məzjan, qad tiit zzərix i tarwanu isin ad 3tamdən ɣifs, iɣin ad kbbərn ẓars. walakin, nik sixfinw, nna jgan mmans, ur ṭṭifx ẓars, awd iʃirri qad iħʃʃəm. ism qattənd isbijn dattisint ism tisint id iʃəlħijn ajd gan. jat luqt, iʃəlħijn ttuħgarn, ṭṭrfən. awd ɣir g lmanasib nɣəd tuɣuri, ħit aʃlħi ixssa adur izri. arn ttafat iḍbibn nɣəd lqoḍat, matalan, hat ɣar a3rabn."

"I did not give my children Amazigh names in order not to make them distinct. As long as a child is in a place which is not his, we have to use the names common in that place. Frankly speaking, it is as if we were not proud of our origin. If I were so attached to our traditions, I would have transmitted them to my children who would keep them and value them. However, I, myself, who is the mother, am not attached to my traditions; therefore; my children would be ashamed of them. The name indicates their identity. The name would reveal that they are Imazighen. Once, Amazigh people were despised and marginalized. In jobs and studies, an Amazigh person should not excel. For example, doctors and judges were only Arabs."

Some parents hold negative attitudes towards the traditional names as they view them as 'outdated' and 'unfashionable'. They believe that these names may not be to the liking of their children once at schools and would make them feel uncomfortable. Some of the informants attribute this phenomenon to the influence of the mass media as people are getting more and more attracted by non-Amazigh names on TV. The following statement, made by a 32-year-old-educated woman, illustrates the extent to which the Amazigh names have become a source of shame for some people.

"ɣuri sin iʃirran, amzwarru giɣas karim, tisnat giɣas salwa. ajnna di zajd karim, innajas umɣar i wrgaz inw adas ng muħa. ur qbilɣ nniɣasn ur as nṭṭəgga ɣir karim. mç as nga muħa çulʃi qad jisin is iga aʃlħij. ur ṛṛiɣ at

ishʃam ism nəs. nkkin s iɣfinw kkixtən ttuħgarɣ aʃçu ism inw iṭṭo. juwn g lʔasatida nw nna urijin aʃlħi ikkatn daj iṭṭini iṭṭo ʃʃəlħa ar ɣifi ṭṭəṣṣan winna d qqarɣ."

"I have two kids. The first one is called karim and the second one Salwa. When Karim was born, my father-in-law asked my husband to name him Moħa. I rejected the idea and I insisted on calling him Karim. In case we called him Moħa, everybody would easily recognize that he is Amazigh. I did not want him to feel ashamed of his name. I myself was despised because my name is Iṭṭo. When I was young, one of my teachers, who was not Amazigh, used to call me Iṭṭo ʃʃəlħa and the students kept laughing at me."

The images portraying Imazighen in the mass media and throughout the Moroccan society have influenced Amazigh people's self perception. The television has been an instrument for displaying stereotypical images about the Amazigh people. They are oftentimes depicted as second-class citizens. They appear on TV programs as ignorant and uncivilized. These stereotypical images have brought about the spread of negative attitudes towards the Amazigh language, its speakers and its culture as whole. Surrounded by stereotypes like these all their lives, some Amazigh people have come to believe them, a thing which has developed in them a sense of inferiority.

The socio-economic mutations Morocco has witnessed since its independence have had a significant impact on the rituals of birth among Ayt Merghad. More specifically, access to the health services, women's literacy, intermarriage, migration and the mass media are major factors that have considerably contributed to the abandoning of a number of practices that were associated with birth among Ayt Merghad.

CONCLUSION

The locus of interest in the present study has been to provide an account of the impact of urbanization and modernization on the Amazigh cultural heritage in Morocco in general and among Ayt Merghad in particular. More specifically, this study was concerned with the investigation of the gradual loss of the Amazigh culture among Ayt Merghad, with a special focus on the rituals of birth. It has also tried to determine the factors behind the disappearance of most of the practices related to these rituals. The comprehensive and detailed understanding of the community's birth rituals both in the pre and post-independence era has allowed the researcher, in turn, to place the findings in a broader perspective. The findings were interpreted with respect to the socio-economic mutations the whole society has witnessed during the last decades.

The findings of the study suggest that the birth rituals were governed by the performance of a number of precautionary measures both during pregnancy and after delivery. Given the high risk of birth complications and infant as well as maternal death, pregnancy and birth were surrounded by superstitions. There was a strong conviction among the members of the community that the evil eye was behind the high mortality rates among mothers and babies during or after delivery. Therefore, birth, as a rite of passage, was characterized by the performance of a set of rites which were performed in order to neutralize its effect. Moreover, the newborn's gender was a determinant factor in the type of celebration to take place. A strong preference for boys was a prevailing aspect of the traditional Ayt Merghad community. This preference was justified by financial, social and psychological reasons. However, in the post-independence era, the reasons behind boys' preference have been weakened. The diversification of the economic activities, the increased rates of girls' schooling and women's access to the job market have shaken the negative attitudes Ayt Merghad used to have towards giving birth to girls.

It was also shown that a number of factor have led to the disappearance of the traditional birth rituals in the Ayt Merghad area. Education, the mass media, intermarriage and migration have all played a major role in changing the Ayt Merghad people's way of thinking and the diffusion of new ideas and practices related to birth. Education and the mass media have had a pivotal role in raising the Ayt Merghad people's awareness about birth-related issues. Besides, contact between the Ayt Merghad community and people from different ethnicities and cultures through intermarriage or migration has also dramatically influenced birth rites in the area. Another key factor behind the loss of the traditional birth rituals is the improvement in the health services in the area. This element has largely influenced the traditional practice in the area.

The changes that the birth rituals witnessed during the last decades are just micro manifestations of macro changes in the community's repertoire of values and mentalities. An understanding of the dynamics of urbanization, globalization and development makes us conclude that the loss of the Amazigh cultural heritage is an inevitable consequence of the modernization process adopted in the whole society. The young generation of the Ayt Merghad community is more open to change and to the influence of globalization. The traditional values and customs of the community are not deeply-rooted in the young's psyche; and the belief and behaviour system of the community is not ingrained in their personality. This makes them more susceptible to the pressure of urbanization and modernization. The young tend to be fascinated by experiencing and adopting new things. Nowadays, most of the Ayt Merghad population has access to global information through the mass media and the internet. This state of affairs has exposed them to new life patterns.

BIBLIOGRAPHY

Alpert, R. (2007). *Women in Morocco: Participation in the Workforce as an Avenue of Social Mobility*. The Moshe Dayan Center for Middle Eastern and African Studies. Tel Aviv University.

Bankole, A., Rodriguez, G. and Westoff, C. (1996). "Mass Media Essages and Reproductive Behavior in Nigeria". *Journal of Biosocial Sciences*, 28(2): 227-239.

Becker, C. (2006). *Amazigh Arts in Morocco: Women Shaping Berber Identity*. Austin: University of Texas Press.

Belghazi, S. and Baden, S. 2002. "Wage Discrimination by Gender in Morocco's Urban Labour Force: Evidence and Implications for Industrial and Labour Policy", in Miller, C. and Vivian, J. (eds.), *Women's Empowerment in the Textile Manufacturing Sectors of Bangladesh and Morocco*. Geneva, Switzerland: UNRISD and UNDP, 35-60.

Bencherifa, A. (1991). *Ecologie Culturelle de l'Oasis du Figuig (Maroc du Nord-Est)*. Montpellier: University Paul Valéry.

Berriane, M., Aderghad, M., Amzil, L., Oussi, A. (2010) "Morocco Country and Research Areas Report". Publications of Mohamed V University and International Migration Institute. Retrieved at May/12/2011 http://www.imi.ox.ac.uk/pdfs/research-projects-pdfs/eumagine-pdfs/eumagine-project-paper-4-morocco-country-and-research-areas-report

Bhardwaj, N., Kukade, J. A., Patil, S. and Bhardwaj, S. (1995). "Randomised Controlled Trial on Modified Squatting Position of Delivery". *Indian Journal of Maternal and Child Health*, 6(2), 33–9.

Blumer, H. (1969). *Symbolic Interactionism: Perspective and Method*. New Jersey: Prentice-Hall, Inc.

Boas, F. (1943). "Recent Anthropology". *Science*, 98, 311-337.

Crohn, J. (1995). *Mixed Matches: How to Create Successful Interracial, Interethnic, and Interfaith Relationships*. New York: Fawcett Columbine.

De Haas, H. (2005). "Morocco's Migration Transition: Trends, Determinants and Future Scenarios". *Global Migration Perspectives research papers series*, No 28. Geneva: Global Commission on International Migration. Retrieved October/8/2012 at

http://www.heindehaas.com/Publications/De%20Haas%202005%20(GCI M%2028)%20Morocco's%20migration%20transition.pdf

De Haas, H. (2007). Turning the Tide? Why Development will not Stop Migration. *Development and Change*, 38(5) 819-840.

Elouizi, M. (2010). "Batailles de Jbel Baddou : Les Cinquante Jours Glorieux". Libération, MAP. Retrieved at November/07/2012 at

http://www.maghress.com/fr/liberation/15592

Gold, R. L. (1997). "The Ethnographic Method in Sociology". Qualitative Inquiry, 3, 388-403.

Hart, D. M. (1978). "Notes on the Sociopolitical Structure and Institutions of TXO Tribes of the Ayt Yafalman Confederacy: The Ayt Murghad and the Ayt Hadidou". In *Revue de L'Occident Musulman et de la Méditerranée*, 26: 55-74.

Hart, D. M. (1981). *Dadda 'Atta and His Forty Grandsons: The Socio-Political Organisation of the Ait Atta of Southern Morocco*. Wisbech, Cambridge shire: MENAS Press.

Hart, D. M. (1984). *The Ait 'Atta of Southern Morocco: Daily Life and Recent History*. Wisbech, Cambridgeshire: MENAS Press.

Hart, D. M. (1985). *Guardians of the Khaibar Pass: the Social Organisation and History of the Afridis of Pakistan*. Vanguard Books.

Hoffman, B. G. (1967). The Structure of Traditional Moroccan Rural Society. The Hague, The Netherlands: Mouton &Co.

Jlok, M. (1993). *La Cérémonie du Mariage en Milieu Ayt Merghad : Essai de Reconstitution de la Cérémonie Traditionnelle.* Rabat: INSAP.

Kabiri, L. (n.d.). "Impact des Changements Climatiques et Anthropiques sur les Ressources en eau dans l'Oasis de Ferkla. (Tinjdad, Goulmima, Errachidia, Maroc". Retrieved March /8/2011 at http://www.unesco.org/mab/doc/mys/2003/kabiri/Report.pdf

Karlsen, S. L., Say, J., Souza, C. J., Hogue, D. L., Calles, A., Gülmezoglu, M. and Raine, R. (2011) "The relationship between Maternal Education and Mortality among Women Giving Birth in Health Care Institutions: Analysis of the Cross Sectional WHO Global Survey on Maternal and Prinatal Health". Retrieved December /3/2011 at http://www.biomedcentral.com/1471-2458/11/606

Kastani, M. (2005). *Alwahat Almaghribiya qabla Alisti3mar "Ghris Namoudajan". [Moroccan Oases before Colonization: the case of Ghris].* Rabat: IRCAM.

Kennedy, R. (2003). *Interracial Intimacies: Sex, Marriage, Identity, and Adoption.* New York: Pantheon.

Khettouch, M. (n.d.). *" Vers L'Epopée de Saghro ".* Retrieved December /10/2012 at http://www.goulmima.com/SAGHRO.doc

Kincaid, D. L. (2000). Social Networks, Ideation, and Contraceptive Bevavior in Bangladesh: A Longitudinal Analysis. Social Science and Medicine 50 (2): 215-231.

LeCompte, M. D., Preissle, J., and Tesch, R. (Eds.). (1993). *Ethnography and Qualitative Design in Educational Research (2nd ed.).* New York: Academic Press.

Lightfoot, D. and Miller, J. A., (1996). "Sijilmassa: The Rise and Fall of a Walled Oasis in Medieval Morocco". *Annals of the Association of American Geographers.* Villanova University, 86 (1): 78-101.

Lincoln, Y. S. and Guba, E. G. (1985). *Naturalistic Inquiry*. Beverly Hills, CA: Sage Publications, Inc.

Llahiane, H., (2004). *Ethnicities, Community Making, and Agrarian Change: The Political Ecology of a Moroccan Oasis*. University Press of America.

Massey, A. (1998). 'The way we Do Things around Here': The Culture of Ethnography. Paper presented at the Ethnography and Education Conference, Oxford University Department of Educational Studies, Oxford.

Mathews, Z. S. (2005). "Birth Rights and Rituals in Rural South India: Care Seeking in the Intrapartum Period". *Journal of Bio-Social Science*, 37(4), 385–411.

Ministère de la Santé (2011). "Santé en Chiffre". Rabat. Maroc : Direction de la Planification et des Etudes Service des Etudes et de l'Information Sanitaire.

Ministère du Plan (1960). Recensement Général de la Population et de l'Habitat. Rabat, Maroc : Direction de la Statistique.

Ministère du Plan (1971). Recensement Général de la Population et de l'Habitat. Rabat, Maroc : Direction de la Statistique.

Ministère du Plan (1982). Recensement Général de la Population et de l'Habitat. Rabat, Maroc : Direction de la Statistique.

Ministère du Plan (1994). Recensement Général de la Population et de l'Habitat. Rabat, Maroc : Direction de la Statistique.

Ministère du Plan (2004). Recensement Général de la Population et de l'Habitat. Rabat, Maroc : Direction de la Statistique.

Peyron, M. (1984). "Contribution à l'Histoire du Haut-Atlas Oriental : les Ayt Yafelman", *Revue de l'Occident musulman et de la Méditerranée*, Vol. 38, 117-135.

Petsonk, J. and Remsen, J. (1988). *Intermarriage Handbook: A Guide for Jews and Christians*. New York: William Marrow.

Piotrow, P. T., Rimon II, J. G., Winnard, K., Kincaid, D.L., Huntington, D. and Convisser, J. (1990). "Mass Media Family Planning Promotion in Three Nigerian Cities". *Studies in Family Planning* 21(5): 265-274.

Roberts, J. and Hanson, L. (2007). "Best Practices in Second Stage Labor Care: Maternal Bearing Down and Positioning". *Journal of Midwifery and Women's Health*, 52(3), 238–45.

Robichez, J., (1946). *Maroc Central*. Editions B. Arthaud, Grenoble-Paris.

Root, M. P. P., (2001). *Loves' Revolution: Interracial Marriage*. Philadelphia: Temple University Press.

Saravanan, S., Turrell, G., Johnson, H. and Fraser, J. (2010). "Birthing Practices of Traditional Birth Attendants in South Asia in the Context of Training Programmes." *Journal of Health Management*, 12, 2: 93–121. SAGE Publications. Los Angeles. London. New Delhi. Singapore. Washington DC. Retrieved November/17/2011 at
http://www.zef.de/module/register/media/08ae_JHM-2010-Sheela%20S.pdf

Shiloh, A., (1961). "The System of Medicine in Middle East Culture." *Middle East Journal* 15, 277–88.

Skelton, T. and Allen, T. (1999). *Culture and Global Change*. London: Routledge.

Skounti, A. (1995). *Le Sang et le Sol. Les Implications Socioculturelles de la Sédentarisation. Cas des Nomades Ayt Merghad*. Thèse de Doctorat. Paris: École des Hautes Études en Sciences Sociales.

Skounti , A. (n.d.) Zaïd Ouskounti, Héros de la Résistance dans le Sud-est du Maroc. Retrieved April/10/2012 at
http://zayduhmad.wordpress.com/tag/zaid-ouhmad/

Spooner, B., (1976). "The Evil Eye in the Middle East." In *The Evil Eye*, ed. C. Maloney. New York: Columbia University Press. 76– 84.

Van Gennep, A., (1960). *Rites of Passage*. London: Routledge.

Westoff, C. F., and Bankole. A (1997). *Mass Media and Reproductive Behavior in Africa*. DHS Analytic Reports. No.2. Calverton, MD: Macro International.

Wilcox, K. (1982). "Ethnography as a Methodology and its Application to the Study of Schooling: a Review". In *Doing the Ethnography of Schooling: Educational Anthropology in Action*, ed. Spindler, G.New York: Holt, Rinehart and Wilson, 15: 456–88.

WHO (1996). 'Care in Normal Birth: A Practical Guide, Report of a Technical Working Group'. Geneva: Maternal and Newborn Health/Safe Motherhood, Division of Reproductive Health, World Health Organisation.

Woods, P. (1994) "Collaborating in Historical Ethnography: Researching Critical Events in Education". *International Journal of Qualitative Studies in Education*, 7, 4, 309-321.

Lightning Source UK Ltd.
Milton Keynes UK
UKHW010659241220
375840UK00002B/372